CURRICULUM UNMASKED

With humour and clarity Mark Roques brings biblical insight to what is taught in our schools. To avoid facing these issues would be to betray our nation's children.

Lyndon Bowring

D0332505

Curriculum Unmasked

Towards
a Christian Understanding of Education

MARK ROQUES
with
Christians in Education

MONARCH

CHRISTIANS IN EDUCATION

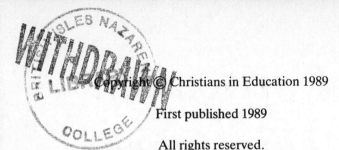

Biblical quotations are from the
New International Version, copyright
© International Bible Society 1973, 1978, 1984.
Anglicisation © 1979, 1984 by Hodder & Stoughton Ltd.

*Front cover photo: The Image Bank
Illustration on page 1 by Joanna Queen*

British Library Cataloguing in Publication Data

Roques, Mark
  Curriculum unmasked.
  1. Great Britain. Education. Christian viewpoints
  I. Title
  261

  ISBN 1–85424–052–8 (Monarch)
       0–7324–0428–2 (Albatross)

Co-published in Australia by
Albatross Books, PO Box 320, Sutherland, NSW 2232

Printed in Great Britain for
MONARCH PUBLICATIONS LTD
1 St Anne's Road, Eastbourne, E Sussex BN21 3UN by
Courier International Ltd., Tiptree, Essex
Typeset by Watermark, Hampermill Cottage, Watford WD1 4PL

CONTENTS

Preface 7

Introduction 9

Part One: The Context of Education

1. A Biblical View of Education 17
2. Idolatry, Enlightenment and the Spirit of Culture
   in the 1980s 43

Part Two: The Textbooks

3. Science 73
4. English 85
5. Mathematics 101
6. Technology 111
7. Geography 115
8. History 121
9. Religious Education 131
10. Art 141

Part Three: A Christian Response

11. Science 153
12. Biology 161
13. History 165
14. Modern Languages 169
15. Geography 177
16. English Literature 183

17.   Economics   189
18.   Specialism in Secondary Schools   195
19.   Team-Teaching and Discipline   203
20.   Avoiding Indoctrination   209
21.   Teaching at Junior and Primary Levels   213
22.   Conclusion   239
Further Reading   251
Christians in Education   254

PREFACE

Christians in Education is a registered charity established to strengthen the position of Christianity in schools, encourage a biblical perspective on education and serve the Christian community in their involvement in education. As we meet parents in local churches around the country, they express concern about the education that their children are receiving. Some parents are asking, 'Why do such seemingly good schools provoke such a negative spiritual attitude in children? Why do my children seem so uninterested in the Christian religion?'

This book is intended to help parents understand something of the education their children receive so that these questions can begin to be answered. To do this we need to unmask the many hidden assumptions of the textbooks that children read. Through the 1988 Education Reform Act the introduction of a National Curriculum, with the possibility of greater uniformity in schools, makes it perhaps easier for Christians to begin to develop an understanding of what is happening in our schools up and down the country. Children and young people are influenced by many different things – parents, pop music, television, comics, friends. But they are also influenced by their teachers and the books they read in school. This book sets out to help parents to understand the unseen assumptions that become part of our children through their education.

It does not attempt to provide an exhaustive analysis of such issues as 'indoctrination' and 'philosophy of education', or provide a detailed proposal as to what must be done to solve some of the problems that are raised. The dominant focus of this book is to unmask the hidden assumptions of curriculum textbooks and to explain what some Christians are doing to respond to this challenge. We are grateful to Mark Roques for the clear and illuminating way he unfolds these issues for us, and also to all those teachers who have been prepared to share their experiences with us in the last section.

The book will also be of help to those teachers and student teachers who wish to integrate their Christian faith with their teaching. Here again a major obstacle to the successful integration of Christianity and education is the presence of a host of assumptions (that are enshrined in school textbooks) that do not permit a radical Christian approach to education.

We hope that this book will be a stimulus and inspiration to teachers as they reflect upon a biblical perspective to the curriculum and see how other teachers have responded to that challenge in their classroom situation.

LYNN MURDOCH
General Director
Christians in Education

INTRODUCTION

As a supply teacher I have taught in many schools. In every school I go to, I meet with the same problem: children and young people who are disillusioned, frustrated and bored. Not all the children I come across feel this way, but a great many do.

'I hate school!'

'It's so borin'.'

'Wish I could go home now.'

'What's the point in doing this, sir?'

'I ain't doing no homework.'

These are common remarks during a typical day. Many of the children I have taught come from broken and painful backgrounds. Marriage breakdown and divorce. Mothers and fathers who have no time for each other, never mind their children. Sexual abuse and incest. Homes where drunken fathers come home late at night and little Tina has made the mistake of being in the way. We are not talking about small problems.

As a supply teacher I often have the unique opportunity to watch and study children.

'Mr Roques, could you please go and supervise 4b. They're a little bit on the rough side so be careful!'

I duly trot along and enjoy 4b. 4b, oozing charm and decorum, greets me:

'Oh, are you a supply teacher, sir?'

'We likes supply teachers, sir.'

'Sean is a fat little pimple and we all hates him, sir. Fat pimple, fat pimple.'

'I hates you Jimmy Baker. I'll get you on the coach.'

'Debra's a fat slag, sir.'

'Jimmy Johnson stinks. Just like his mum.'

Cruel teasing and mockery seem to be the order of the day. The mood changes of some children are, at times, quite staggering to behold. At one moment two smiling children seem entranced with each other: joy and laughter fill the room. Suddenly a cacophony of shouting and swearing erupts as little Brenda screams with rage as little Frank wrenches her neck into a position he prefers. Of course, I do not want to claim that all children behave like this. That would be quite mistaken. My experience has mostly been in secondary schools. The situation in many primary schools is different. Most primary and junior school children experience life as meaningful and hopeful. But it seems to me that a sense of futility and despair increases as you go from first to fifth year in secondary school. One of the central purposes of this book is to explore precisely what contributes to this lack of purpose and hope.

For many teachers it has become almost impossible to teach; it requires so much energy and skill merely to control the class. Numerous newspaper articles and reports document the rising levels of violence and disruptive behaviour in schools.[1]

Talking with many young people in schools, I have had the overwhelming sense that life is harsh, painful and meaningless for them. For many, education is simply a means to an end: getting a job – perhaps. There is little idealism or optimism; the future is uncertain and anxiety provoking.

What does the living God feel about this? How does Jesus Christ, the Prince of Peace and Saviour of the entire cosmos, respond? I believe that Jesus weeps when he sees such brokenness and hopelessness. We know from the New Testament that Jesus loved children: 'Let the little children come to me, and do not hinder them, for the kingdom of God belongs to such as these. I tell you the truth, anyone who will not receive the kingdom of God like a little child will never enter it. And he took the children in his arms, put his hands on them and blessed them' (Mk 10:14–16).

Here we see the King of Creation hugging children! Many other passages in Scripture speak of God's love and concern for children. The prophet Isaiah says:

The wolf will live with the lamb,
the leopard will lie down with the goat,
the calf and the lion and the yearling together;
and a little child will lead them.
The cow will feed with the bear,
their young will lie down together,
and the lion will eat straw like the ox.
The infant will play near the hole of the cobra,
and the young child put his hand into the viper's nest.
They will neither harm nor destroy
on all my holy mountain,
for the earth will be full of the knowledge of the Lord
as the waters cover the sea.

(Isaiah 11:6–9)

This is a marvellous picture of how God really wanted his world to be. Notice the sense of refreshment, joy and peace. How incredible that wolves and lambs should be the best of friends and children can play with snakes. Sadly this contrasts very bitterly with present experience. In the Scriptures we catch glimpses of God's creation liberated from bondage, misery and death – and it is simply fantastic. But we know that right now the creation is groaning with pain. Paul tells us that 'the creation waits in eager expectation for the sons of God to be revealed. For the creation was subjected to frustration, not by its own choice, but by the will of the one who subjected it, in hope that the creation itself will be liberated from its bondage to decay and brought into the glorious freedom of the children of God' (Romans 8:19–21).

The Lord God Yahweh longs to save and heal his broken world. It is for this reason that he cares about children.

In this book I want to look at the context in which children are being educated in the 1980s. What is actually going on in many schools up and down our country? We must realise that children are being profoundly affected by the education they receive and the answers they are being given to four important questions:

1 What is the world like?
2 What is wisdom and knowledge?
3 What is a human being?
4 What is happiness and well being?

We will first look at how the Bible answers these questions. Then we will look at how modern secular culture tends to answer them, and how it influences and shapes children. After exploring these primary issues, we will investigate some of the textbooks that our children read in schools, concentrating on those subjects that the National Curriculum refers to as 'core' and 'foundation' subjects. We will also look at religious education which is part of the basic curriculum of schools. This will help us to understand a secular approach to the curriculum. What answers do these textbooks give, explicitly and implicitly, to our four questions? Finally, we will investigate the constructive and exciting contribution Christians are making in the field of curriculum.

Before we go any further, let me explain what I mean by the word 'curriculum'. A curriculum is the combined content of all the different subjects normally taught in schools. How do we teach biology, maths, chemistry, history, French, RE, etc? And how do these subjects hang together? These are curriculum questions. In the light of the recently proposed National Curriculum, such issues are increasingly becoming of great public concern. It is my hope that this book will stimulate and encourage Christians to think and reflect about education and curriculum.

Note

1. One such report, entitled 'Discipline in Schools', was published by the Professional Association of Teachers. It reads as follows:

   The Association's Position

   2.1 The Association's present position on the subject of school discipline arises from the overwhelming support given at its Annual Conference at the University of Exeter in 1987 to a motion expressing concern about the rising incidence of violence and indiscipline in schools.

   2.2 As a result of this expression of concern, a questionnaire was sent to all members on the subject. No fewer than 94% of those who responded said they believed that indiscipline was on the increase in schools.

   2.3 In November of last year, the executive committee of the Association resolved to ask the Prime Minister to establish an enquiry into discipline in schools throughout the United Kingdom. The following statement was made to the press at the same time: 'In schools up and down the country, a few disruptive and aggressive children are bringing the education process to a halt in lesson after lesson. The ordinary child, who just wants to get on with learning, is rapidly becoming the most neglected individual in the education system. Unless the problem of indiscipline and violence in schools is dealt with, there will soon be none prepared to teach and none able to learn in the nation's schools.'

Part One

The Context
of Education

CHAPTER ONE

A BIBLICAL VIEW OF EDUCATION

1. What is the world like?

> The heavens declare the glory of God;
> the skies proclaim the work of his hands.
> Day after day they pour forth speech;
> night after night they display knowledge.
> There is no speech or language
> where their voice is not heard.
> Their voice goes out into all the earth,
> their words to the ends of the world.
> In the heavens he has pitched a tent for the sun,
> which is like a bridegroom
> coming forth from his pavilion,
> like a champion rejoicing to run his course.
> It rises at one end of the heavens
> and makes its circuit to the other;
> nothing is hidden from its heat.
>
> Psalm 19:1–6

In this psalm we can see clearly that the world reveals the majesty and splendour of the living God. Just think of all the amazing creatures God has made! Scripture tells us that the sun is a servant of the Lord; yes, in some inexplicable way that burning, yellow sun is responding to the King of kings. Picture it. You're walking home after a dinner party and you catch a couple of stars winking at you. You look upwards and see hundreds and hundreds of these creatures doing their own thing. It's an incredible experience. I remember once years ago coming home from church late one evening. It had been snowing and I was in the mood for serious and committed slumber. And then I caught the stars twinkling and making merry. For the first time I began to understand Psalm 19: 'Day after day they pour forth speech; night after night they display knowledge.' Those stars were declaring to me the greatness of God.

Creation is very colourful and richly diverse. It is a revelation of the true God who made it. So any curriculum that is faithful to God must reflect this colourful richness. Let's have a look at one more psalm.

> How many are your works, O Lord!
> In wisdom you made them all;
> the earth is full of your creatures.
> There is the sea, vast and spacious,
> teeming with creatures beyond number –
> living things both large and small.
> There the ships go to and fro,
> and the leviathan, which you formed to frolic there.
>
> Psalm 104:24–26

This passage tells us that God formed the leviathan to frolic in the ocean. We do not know precisely what the leviathan was. Perhaps a whale, or a huge crocodile. Who can say? But we do know from Scripture that leviathan was a huge creature and that he enjoyed a good frolic!

As twentieth-century Christians we need to recapture the vital vision of Psalm 104. The Lord God delights in the world he has made. He created the earth by his power; he founded the world by his wisdom and stretched out the heavens by his understanding (Jer 10:12). God has poured so much of his beauty, genius and flair into the works of his hands and it is crucial that a biblically founded curriculum reflect this. Take the dolphin, for example. Those animals seem to be perpetually smiling. They glide through the water with consummate ease and they have even saved drowning sailors by carrying them into shallow water. All this proclaims the wonder of our God. As the prophet Isaiah says:

> You will go out in joy
> and be led forth in peace;
> the mountains and hills
> will burst into song before you,
> and all the trees of the field
> will clap their hands.
>
> Isaiah 55:12

The trees, the mountains, the hills, the valleys, the ravines, the animals, the stars and the sun are all praising the name of the Lord! As creatures of God, they know who they are. In some way God's world sings to him. Job tells us this:

> But ask the animals, and
> they will teach you,
> or the birds of the air, and
> they will tell you;
> or speak to the earth, and it
> will teach you,
> or let the fish of the sea inform you.
> Which of all these does not know
> that the hand of the Lord has done this?
> In his hand is the life of every creature
> and the breath of all mankind.
>
> Job 12:7–10

God's world is alive and enchanted. It is charged with his grandeur. It is the very theatre of his glory. The book of Proverbs puts it like this:

> The Lord possessed me at
> the beginning of his work,
> before his deeds of old;
> I was appointed from eternity,
> from the beginning, before the world began.
> When there were no oceans,

I was given birth,
when there were no springs abounding with water;
before the mountains were settled in place,
before the hills, I was given birth,
before he made the earth or its fields
or any of the dust of the world.
I was there when he set the heavens in place,
when he marked out the horizon
on the face of the deep,
when he established the clouds above
and fixed securely the fountains of the deep,
when he gave the sea its boundary
so the waters would not overstep his command,
and when he marked out the foundations of the earth.
Then I was the craftsman at his side.
I was filled with delight day after day,
rejoicing always in his presence,
rejoicing in his whole world
and delighting in mankind.

Proverbs 8:22–31

This passage tells us that God delights in the earth and all the creatures that inhabit the earth. Of course he rejoices over men and women, but he also delights in all the other creatures he has made.

When we can see with the eyes of faith that God's many creatures reveal the majesty, glory, and splendour of the King of kings, we are not tempted to worship the created. Only a fool will say to an otter or a giraffe: you are divine, we worship you. Nor will we rob such creatures of their splendour by pretending that they are emotionless machines as some secular philosophers have thought. We will neither worship nor vilify such animals. Instead we will thank God that he has made such a fantastic creation.

Children and young people need to see that this world we inhabit is the stunning playground of our Father in heaven. We must not allow our children to lose this sense of mystery as they gaze at Ron the porcupine or Ralph the badger. So much secular theory would have us believe that God's world is nothing but a bundle of perceptions or a mass of lonely molecules. A world created by the power of mens' minds. But if our children learn this, how can they delight in the living God who made the heavens and the earth by his power and wisdom?

A Christian approach to knowledge and curriculum must take seriously the richness and coherence of God's world. Our theories in maths, history, geography, physics, art, etc., must reflect insight into our Father's rainbow-rich, multi-faceted cosmos. Why? Simply because all these subjects deal with God's world. We will see precisely how a little later.

Before we turn to our second question, it might be helpful to explain what I mean by coherence. We have some sense now of the richness and colour of God's world, but what about its coherence? The book of Colossians throws some light on this: 'He is the image of the invisible God, the firstborn over all creation. For by him all things were created: things in heaven and on earth, visible and invisible, whether thrones or powers or rulers or authorities; all things were created by him and for him. He is before all things, and in him all things hold together' (Col 1:15–17).

This passage refers to the Prince of Peace, Jesus Christ. All things in heaven and on earth (crocodiles, duck-billed platypuses, ferrets, dandelions, tulips, apricots, diamonds, pearls, oil, gas, seaweed, spinach, French and Spanish, emotions, thoughts, imagination, art, education, eyes, legs, hair, humour, wit, angels, little boys and girls, men and women, frogs and snails etc.) were created for Jesus Christ and by Jesus Christ.[1] Not only that, all things hold together in Jesus Christ! Jesus makes everything make sense. That's what we mean by coherence.

When we look at God's world we can see a beautiful cosmos; granted it is a universe polluted by sin and satanic activity, but a beautiful cosmos nonetheless. This cosmos is not meaningless. It is ordered and structured with wisdom and variety. We could say that this world is structured by God's laws. Koala bears were fashioned in a certain way by the Father for Jesus Christ. They are not elephants! A curriculum which wishes to honour the Bible and the world God has made must respect the richness, colour, coherence and lawfulness of Christ's creation. A curriculum, sensitive to the biblical vision will promote integration; different spheres and areas of life will not be presented as fragmented and unconnected. Maths, art, history, biology and economics are not isolated lonely 'subjects'; they speak to us of a multi-faceted and integrated creation.

2. What is wisdom?

Let us turn now to our second question: what is wisdom? Any school worth its name is concerned to impart wisdom and knowledge to its pupils. Teachers are very fond of saying that a certain child knows a great deal; Boris knows a lot for his age; Jenny thinks she knows a lot but she doesn't really. Such comments are frequent when teachers get together. What is this thing called knowledge? And what is this thing called wisdom? Christian reflection on curriculum and education needs to probe these questions.

Let's start by listening to Scripture:

> Does not wisdom call out?
> Does not understanding raise her voice?
> On the heights along the way,
> where the paths meet, she takes her stand;
> beside the gates leading into the city,
> at the entrances, she cries aloud:
> To you, O men, I call out;
> I raise my voice to all mankind.
> You who are simple, gain prudence;
> you who are foolish, gain understanding.
> Listen, for I have worthy things to say;
> I open my lips to speak what is right,

My mouth speaks what is true,
for my lips detest wickedness.
All the words of my mouth are just;
none of them is crooked or perverse.
To the discerning all of them are right;
they are faultless to those who have knowledge.
Choose my instruction instead of silver,
knowledge rather than choice gold,
for wisdom is more precious than rubies,
and nothing you desire can compare with her.

Proverbs 8:1–11

Wisdom, understanding and knowledge, when rooted in the fear and love of God, bring wholeness and peace to those who seek them. Wisdom brings life in all its fullness. Folly, wisdom's opposite, brings death in all its emptiness. Christian education must seek to impart wisdom and understanding to children. Wisdom opens children up to God's greatness and beauty and to the splendour of his creation. But we need to see that wisdom covers a great deal more than many Christians have supposed.

Scripture speaks of wisdom and knowledge in many different ways. Let's look at a few of them: 'See, I have taught you decrees and laws as the Lord my God commanded me, so that you may follow them in the land you are entering to take possession of it. Observe them carefully, for this will show your wisdom and understanding to the nations, who will hear about all these decrees and say, "Surely this great nation is a wise and understanding people"' (Deut 4:5–7).

This passage shows us that wisdom in the Scripture is intimately connected to obeying God's laws and decrees. God revealed his laws to his people at Mount Sinai, and of course the ten commandments are a very important part of the law. But there is a great deal more to the law than just the ten commandments. In Exodus, Leviticus and Deuteronomy there are many laws that pertain to farming, finance, justice for the poor, orphans and widows, sexuality, parties, celebrations, treatment of animals and the land, healthy diets, and more besides. All these laws reveal wisdom and understanding because they bring life, wholeness and 'shalom' (peace) to those who respond to their wisdom and obey them.

For example, God told his people to have a year long holiday once every seven years (Leviticus chapter 25). He commanded them not to work at all for a whole year! He also told them to let the animals have a rest as well. Not only this, the Lord also told his people to cancel all debts and release all slaves in that seventh year (Deuteronomy chapter fifteen). Tired workers, exhausted servants and weary oxen would have a complete rest from their labours. The land too could breathe deeply and be replenished. Destitute men and women would be relieved of oppressive debt and slaves would be freed. We can see that God's laws and ways restore people, animals and the land to health and wholeness. They bring joy and shalom to a broken, groaning world. Wisdom in the Bible is intimately related to God's ways of justice, righteousness, faithfulness and compassion. And Jesus came to fulfil all these wise laws (Mt 5:17).[2]

In Scripture the wise person is someone who so meditates on God's ways, decrees and statutes that he or she begins to delight in the true meaning of the law. The Christian community needs to recapture this insight because it has phenomenal implications for every aspect of our lives. Let's take an example. In Leviticus chapter 19 verses 9–10 God told his people to glean. This meant that he didn't want the average farmer to harvest all the food he possibly could from his land. Instead our farmer friend was meant to leave quite a bit of corn or wheat at the edges of his plot of land; this would mean that Brian and Tina, an unemployed couple from the suburbs of Jericho, would be able to obtain some decent food without having to beg or steal. If we continue our meditation we will find more surprises. Gleaning, if obeyed, would have demanded longer tea- and lunch-breaks. Why, you might ask? Well, it has been estimated that the practice of gleaning would have reduced the work load by twenty per cent!

Imagine the following scenario. A fine summer's day, the sky azure, the bees busy about the Lord's work – making honey. Ron and Milly are enjoying an extended lunch-break (a light lunch – chicken salad washed down with a local vino). A widow, Maud, and her young daughter, Ethel, are gleaning in the far corner of the field. They have recently become destitute and they are feeling none too cheerful. Milly, who loves God and life, has just been thinking about the law. She begins to catch its true meaning, gasps with new-found pleasure, and calls over to Maud and Ethel. 'Fancy a spot of lunch? We've got plenty to spare.' Peace and justice have entered that field. This is precisely the kind of scenario that God loves. In actual fact, a very similar situation to this is described in the Book of Ruth. God's law opens us up to seeing that doing justice and having fun can be successfully combined if done God's way. There are many other delightful surprises in God's law if you have the eyes to see them.[3]

Wisdom relates to many different kinds of activity. There is of course wisdom in the way that wise parents raise their children (Proverbs 13). But there are many other kinds of wisdom as well. Let us run through a few of them briefly.

> Listen and hear my voice;
> pay attention and hear what I say.
> When a farmer plows for planting, does he
> plow continually?
> Does he keep on breaking up and harrowing the soil?
> When he has levelled the surface,
> does he not sow caraway and scatter cummin?
> Does he not plant wheat in its place,
> barley in its plot,
> and spelt in its field?
> His God instructs him
> and teaches him the right way.
>
> Caraway is not threshed with a sledge,
> nor is a cartwheel rolled over cummin;
> caraway is beaten out with a rod,

> and cummin with a stick.
> Grain must be ground to make bread;
> so one does not go on threshing it for ever.
> Though he drives the wheels of his threshing cart
> over it, his horses do not grind it.
> All this also comes from the Lord Almighty,
> wonderful in counsel and magnificent in wisdom.
>
> Isaiah 28:23–29

We have already seen that there is a great deal in the law which speaks to us about farming – the sabbatical laws demanded that the land should be rested one year in seven. Isaiah deepens our understanding of this by revealing to us that obedient farming requires wisdom and that this wisdom comes from the Lord. A farmer can find the path of agricultural wisdom if he or she listens to the voice of God. There is a peculiar kind of wisdom that the wise farmer possesses. It is not an academic wisdom, it is an agricultural wisdom.

The Book of Kings tells us about a different kind of wisdom.

> When the queen of Sheba saw all the wisdom of Solomon and the palace he had built ... she was overwhelmed.
>
> She said to the King, 'The report I heard in my own country about your achievements and your wisdom is true. But I did not believe these things until I came and saw with my own eyes. Indeed, not even half was told me; in wisdom and wealth you have far exceeded the report I heard ... Because of the Lord's eternal love for Israel, he has made you king, to maintain justice and righteousness.' (1 Kings 10:4–9).

Solomon was gifted with a peculiar kind of wisdom that could discern justice. He was a king (before he fell away) who knew that a king is called to do justice (see Psalm 72). This is a different kind of wisdom from agricultural wisdom. It goes without saying that a biblical view of knowledge and education should make young children sensitive to issues of justice. The Lord wants children who are compassionate and willing to speak up on behalf of the oppressed (Isaiah 58 and James 5).

To these four young men God gave knowledge and understanding of all kinds of literature and learning. And Daniel could understand visions and dreams of all kinds.

At the end of the time set by the king to bring them in, the chief official presented them to Nebuchadnezzar. The king talked with them, and he found none equal to Daniel, Hananiah, Mishael and Azariah; so they entered the king's service. In every matter of wisdom and understanding about which the king questioned them, he found them ten times better than all the magicians and enchanters in his whole kingdom.

Daniel 1:17–20

Here we can detect at least two different kinds of wisdom. On the one hand there is a kind of scholarly or literary wisdom which is very pleasing to the Lord if done in service to him. On the other hand there is a different kind of wisdom vis a vis the interpretation of visions and dreams. We might call this spiritual knowing. We should remember that both kinds of wisdom are equally valid.

> My son, pay attention to my wisdom,
> listen well to my words of insight,
> that you may maintain discretion and
> your lips may preserve knowledge.
> For the lips of an adulteress drip honey,
> and her speech is smoother than oil;
> but in the end she is bitter as gall,
> sharp as a double-edged sword.

Proverbs 5:1–4

There is another kind of wisdom which we might call ethical or moral wisdom. It is important for children to develop their moral sensitivity and to ground this in the fear of the Lord (Proverbs 9:10). A great deal needs to be said about this. I will restrict myself to a few brief comments.

In the Book of Proverbs there is a very clear distinction between right and wrong conduct. Adultery is presented as offensive to God and faithfulness as pleasing. To keep such commandments requires wisdom. We could call such wisdom ethical or moral wisdom. Such wisdom is more precious than rubies; more valuable than fine gold. Children need to understand that stealing and cruelty for example is offensive to God. The biblical perspective gives us a clear sense of right and wrong.

It also needs to be noted that moral wisdom should always be taught in conjunction with the other kinds of wisdom. If you open children up to fun, laughter, joy, sensitivity, wholeness and artistic knowing, etc., it is much easier to help them understand the importance of such moral issues as sexual fidelity and telling the truth. Many well-meaning Christian parents have gone through the awful experience of raising children to hold good 'morals' only to find that their children rebel against these values. This is often because they have not understood the creational context within which morality makes sense. Being righteous makes perfect sense within the context of God's justice and shalom. We do not want our children to be only righteous. We want them to be children who think clearly and have great imagination; children who can be playful and appropriately cheeky; children who are not tiny scheming Pharisees but children who are whole and can entertain us for hours with their lovable pranks. If you do not affirm the goodness of God's creation to young children then they will probably rebel against you, however high your 'morals'. Children, just like us, need to taste and see that God is good and that walking in his ways brings wholeness, peace and integration.

A careful reading of both the Old and New Testament reveals many different types of wisdom and understanding. Space does not permit us to examine them all here. The following are a few references. Exodus 35:30–35 tells us about the wisdom and skill of artists and craftsmen. 1 Kings 5:29–34 speaks of the wisdom of poets, musicians, biologists and botanists. Proverbs 31:10-31 tells us about the wisdom of a business-woman. And so we could go on and on.

Christians need to recapture the radically biblical insight

that all wisdom is hidden in Jesus Christ. Paul wrote about this in his letter to the Colossians:

> I want you to know how much I am struggling for you and for those at Laodicea, who have not met me personally. My purpose is that they may be encouraged in heart and united in love, so that they may have the full riches of complete understanding, in order that they may know the mystery of God, namely, Christ, in whom are hidden all the treasures of wisdom and knowledge.
>
> Colossians 2:1–3

In all of life, whether farming, business, education, raising a family, scholarship, art, managing a football club, politics, technology or marriage, the Scriptures continually drive home the same point: you can either follow wisdom or folly. Life or death. Now, many Christians will grant the point that Christ's wisdom is essential for a healthy marriage or family – but farming? What does Christ have to do with that? But this objection fails to acknowledge that the entire cosmos belongs to Jesus Christ and all wisdom and knowledge is somehow rooted in him.[4]

The biblical view of wisdom and knowledge is much richer than that of our secular culture. For many people wisdom and knowledge can be reduced to a brute familiarity with 'facts' and a narrow range of technical skills. But wisdom in the Bible concerns an empathy and love for that which is known. For example, the wisdom of a therapist requires emotional sensitivity; we might even speak of emotional wisdom.

3. What is a human being?

It seems to me that any approach to education will presuppose answers to this question. Some people have believed that people are not what they seem to be at all. They are really rational immortal souls who are imprisoned inside evil bodies. These rational souls do not belong in this world of colour and diversity; they belong in heaven where they can discuss maths and philosophy for ever and ever. This may seem quite dreadful to us but many ancient people and some modern people still believe it. In Plato's *Phaedo*, for example, Socrates speaks of heaven as a place where philosophers will discuss philosophy with the gods. This place is unsullied by bodies, emotions and sexual desire. Only intelligible and rational entities will exist in that place. Earthly existence is understood as imprisonment. The rational soul is imprisoned within the body as a bird is locked up in a cage.

Now if you take this line of thought, curriculum and educational practice will be adapted accordingly. Teachers will be concerned to help their children prepare for their heavenly future where bodies, feelings, jokes, trees, marbles, stoats and ferrets don't crop up. You don't need to be very bright to realise that this view of what it means to be human will demand a curriculum that is very hot on arithmetic, geometry and logic. And very little else.

Other people believe that human beings are simply clever animals who have a genius for survival. Unlike those who believe that we used to be rational souls living in heaven and it would be rather nice if we returned to that state, these people tend to believe that we used to be tiny primitive organisms and we would prefer not to go back to that state! As highly evolved survival-machines, we would prefer to become ever more efficient survival-machines. This view results in a curriculum that depends heavily upon a very pragmatic science and technology. Science and technology courses that will help you to survive and cope in a harsh and hostile environment. Sound familiar?[5]

What does the Bible say about what it means to be human?

O Lord, our Lord, how majestic is your name
in all the earth!
You have set your glory above the heavens.
From the lips of children and infants
you have ordained praise because of your enemies,
to silence the foe and the avenger.

When I consider your heavens,
the work of your fingers, the moon and the stars,
which you have set in place,
what is man that you are mindful of him,
the son of man that you care for him?
You made him a little lower than the heavenly beings
and crowned him with glory and honour.
You made him ruler over the works of your hands;
you put everything under his feet: all flocks and herds,
and the beasts of the field,
the birds of the air, and the fish of the sea,
all that swim the paths of the seas.
O Lord, our Lord, how majestic is your name in
all the earth!

Psalm 8

In this psalm we can see that men and womens' lives are full of significance and meaning. They are 'crowned with glory and honour'. A slightly more promising view of humanity than the two views we have just sketched! Each person in the world is of infinite worth; all men, women and children are stunning creatures because the King of kings, Jesus Christ, has crowned them with glory and honour. Not only this; men and women were created to rule over the works of God's hands. We were made by Jesus Christ and for Jesus Christ for an incredible purpose. God created you and me to be stewards and lords of the rest of creation. He wanted the human race to care for and tenderly develop the rest of creation, not abuse and torture and destroy it. Right from the very beginning, God wanted his special creatures, humans, to love him with all their hearts, minds and souls and to love each other. This task included subduing the earth.

To gain greater insight into what this means we need to go back to the very beginning of the Bible. In Genesis chapter 1 God makes it pretty clear that he was having a ball when he made the heavens and the earth. He was positively enjoying himself – no holds barred. God made the land and he saw that it was good. God made the sea and saw that it was good. God made the ferret and saw that it was good. God made the cashew-nut and saw that it was good. This conveys the tone of Genesis 1. The entire creation was filled with the glory and presence of God. All in all it was a jewel of a cosmos and a lot of lasting friendships were being made. And then we get to verse 26: 'Then God said, "Let us make man in our image, in our likeness, and let them rule over the fish of the sea and the birds of the air, over the livestock, over all the earth, and over all the creatures that move along the ground." So God created man in his own image, in the image of God he created him; male and female he created them. God blessed them and said to them, "Be fruitful and increase in number; fill the earth and subdue it. Rule over the fish of the sea and the birds of the air and over every living creature that moves on the ground."'

When God gets to this point of making human creatures, he becomes very eloquent, almost loquacious. The King of kings has been moulding and shaping his world with power and wisdom and then he gets to us. God, who is the great and mighty King, makes us in his image so that we can exercise dominion over his world. He calls us to image him by continuing his act of creation. He wants us to open up and develop his creation. What do I mean by this?

Let's briefly examine Genesis chapter 2: 'The Lord God took the man and put him in the Garden of Eden to work it and take care of it' (Gen 2:15).

This is an important biblical theme and intensely relevant to education. In fact it is crucial to the entire thrust of what education is all about. This important verse helps us to understand precisely how we are meant to subdue the earth. God does not say, 'Destroy as much of the garden as you can and I'll pop back in a few hours to see how you are doing.' Quite the reverse is intended by this verse. In the original Hebrew two words are used for 'work' and 'take care of'; these words are *abad* and *shamar*. Human responsibility and care for the earth are very much implied by these two words. Loren

Wilkinson puts it like this:

> The first of these verbs, 'abad', is often translated 'till', but it is
> sometimes translated 'work' or 'serve'. And in fact, 'abad' is the
> basic Hebrew word for 'serve' or even 'be a slave to'. The other
> word, 'shamar', is translated variously 'keep', 'watch', or 'pre-
> serve'. The significant thing about both words is that they describe
> actions undertaken not primarily for the sake of the doer, but for
> the sake of the object of the action. The kind of tilling which is to
> be done is a service of the earth. The keeping of the garden is not
> just for human comfort, but is a kind of preservation. Both verbs
> severely restrict the way the other two verbs – subdue and rule –
> are to be applied. Human ruling, then, should be exercised in such
> a way as to serve and preserve the beasts, the trees, the earth itself
> – all of which is being ruled.[6]

These remarks from Wilkinson help us to see that humans
are indeed called to exercise dominion over the earth; we are
called to mould, shape and develop creation, but we are called
to do this task in a way that reflects God's tender rule of justice, mercy and faithfulness. We are not lawless masters of an
inanimate, lifeless 'nature'. We are stewards of God's rich and
colourful world and we are called to obey his laws. Leviticus
chapter 25 makes it abundantly clear that respect for the land
and the animals is as much a part of God's law as refusing to
commit adultery with your neighbour's spouse.

A Christian approach to education and the curriculum
should earnestly convey to young people that this task of
stewardship and respect for God's laws and ways can be a
positive delight. We should never restrict the scope of God's
concern for all creation. We must continually stress the
beauty and wholeness of God's ways, for they bring life and
blessing. We must beware of the leaven of the Pharisees and
the Sadducees because it hides the beauty and the relevance
of the law from the ordinary person. These contemporary
priests of Jesus tended to ignore those important parts of the
law which spoke of God's love for the oppressed, the orphans,
the destitute, the broken-hearted, not to mention God's love

and concern for his animals and his land (see Matthew 23:23). Jesus enraged the Pharisees and the Sadducees by reminding them of laws that they were reluctant to mention and unwilling to obey. In Luke chapter 4, verse 19, when he speaks of the acceptable year of the Lord (Lev 25; Is 49:8–9), Jesus proclaims to these priests that the law commanded the rich to return land to the landless. Rich and complacent priests would have found this difficult to stomach.

There is so much more to this biblical idea of stewardship than one might at first expect. For example, when the Lord placed Adam and Eve in the Garden, he invited them to be its gardeners. But do you think that God only wanted Adam and Eve to plant turnips, mangoes, yams and strawberries for eternity? Of course not. I have the greatest respect for such delicious fruit and veg. But to be a steward of creation involves a great deal more than just planting and harvesting.

When God created the cosmos, he did not only make air, water, soil, rocks, plants, animals, humans and angels. The Lord, being extraordinarily brilliant, witty and inventive, also created millions and millions of amazing possibilities. For example, if you purse your lips and blow, you will begin to whistle. A possibility in the creation is opened up. God wanted men and women to *develop civilisation and culture to the praise of his name*. In Genesis 4 we see human beings developing the potential of creation. These innovative people were responding to God's command to develop civilisation and culture. An imaginary story may help to clarify this exciting biblical theme.

Picture it. Adam and Eve are walking through the Garden. Lions, gazelles, pumas and armadillos are prancing around doing impressions of each other. Suddenly Adam's roving eye espies a mango tree and the happy couple proceed in its direction. As they approach the tree, Adam becomes uncomfortably aware that they will not be able to taste this unforbidden fruit – the mangoes are far too high up to be picked. But Eve pipes up: 'Hang on, Adam me old fruit, just let me subdue the

earth a bit and we'll soon be enjoying yonder luscious fruit.'
Eve's powerful intellect surges into top gear and before you
can say 'piranas like to eat you' she has come up with the perfect solution. Eve stoops down, selects a suitable branch lying
on the ground, bends it so, twists it there, and produces a suitable tool by which to purloin the required fruit. Sinking his
teeth into his mango, Adam praises God for this possibility,
discovered by his clever wife, and suggests to Eve that they
call this new fruit a banana. Eve feels uncomfortable with this
name and a friendly and playful debate ensues. Finally they
agree to call this new fruit a mango.[7]

Adam and Eve have just been subduing the earth – and having a lot of fun while at it. They have begun to develop very
primitive culture and civilisation and they have also been
entertaining God and his angels. Do you see what they've
accomplished? Eve was doing quite a bit of thinking and
designing; she was opening up the creational possibilities of
thought and primitive technology. Adam and Eve named the
mango a mango, after considerable tomfoolery. Language
and humour were being unfolded.

The Book of Genesis tells us how the descendents of Adam
and Eve responded to God's command to develop culture and
civilisation. In Genesis chapter 4 Tubal-Cain 'forged all kinds
of instruments out of bronze and iron'. Jubal, the brother of
Jabal, developed the very first harps and flutes. And this is the
glory of humanity – we shape and mould, we develop and
unfold. The earth is pregnant with possibility and we are commanded to bring forth this potential.

Let us remember that such unfolding of creational possibilities is not only pleasing to God, it is expected. The Bible
begins with a garden but ends with a city (Rev 21). Wise and
obedient cultural formation is something God commands us
to do. In educational terms, the Lord wants children to
explore, investigate and develop his creation – and he wants
them to take delight in this. Why? Because he does and he
made us in his image. But it is crucial that children explore the

creation in ways that please the Lord. They must develop sensitivity to his ways of integrity, compassion, justice, stewardship, love and righteousness. We know with great sadness and chagrin that many people are exploring, investigating and tormenting God's precious creation in ways that make him extremely angry. The Book of Revelation tells us that 'those who practise magic arts, the sexually immoral, the murderers, the idolaters and everyone who loves and practises falsehood' (Rev 22:15) will not enter the Holy City, the New Jerusalem. Revelation also tells us that God will destroy those who destroy the earth (Rev 11:18).

While it is true that God calls us to this meaningful task of developing and stewarding the creation, the reality of sin and brokenness surrounds us. Frustration, irritation and violence infect and distort our response to God. The reality of the fall dulls and embitters our beauty. Tragically, we are stewards in desperate need of redemption, servants and explorers of creation who are lost in sin and darkness. As humans we develop cities, farms, machines, language, pottery. As men and women, made in the image of God, we shape and mould God's world, but our rebellion against him distorts and wounds our civilisations. We are stewards, servant-lords of his world, but we are also ensnared by sin and death. Perhaps we could say that the Bible reveals to us that humans are wonderful but broken servants of God.

Scripture clearly shows us that the creation is cursed by sin. Rebellion against our Creator has infected humans and the earth. Weeds and thistles frustrate the farmer; men dominate and oppress women; earthquakes terrify entire cities. Man and land is in bondage to the kingdom of darkness and Satan. We are stewards who need the 'Lamb of God' to redeem us, forgive us and empower us.

Education that pleases the God of the Bible must implicitly and explicitly present human beings as stewards of the Lord's world. The whole person stands before the face of God and will be answerable to him on the day of judgement. The dominant pagan view of a human being was coloured by a hatred of this world as intrinsically worthless (Gnosticism and Neo-Platonism), encouraging an escapist attitude. The dominant secular view often understands a human being as a survival-machine that must cope with a harsh and demanding world; man becomes a harsh master of his environment. Both these positions reject the biblical view that humans are stewards of God's creation and subject to his life-giving laws.

4. What is happiness or well-being?

> Blessed are you who are poor,
> for yours is the kingdom of God.
> Blessed are you who hunger now,
> for you will be satisfied.
> Blessed are you who weep now,
> for you will laugh.
> Blessed are you when men hate you,
> when they exclude you and insult you
> and reject your name as evil,
> because of the Son of Man.
>> Luke 6:20–22

As Christians we believe that Jesus, the Prince of Peace, came into this world to redeem men and women who had broken the eternal covenant. He suffered and died upon the cross and after three days rose from the dead. Why did he do this? The Lord tells us that he did this for us and the rest of creation because he so loved the world (John 3:16). His sacrifice atones for our sins. God's judgment is poured out upon this perfect King so that we may be forgiven; our sins cast into the very depths of the sea. Through the death and resurrection of the Lamb of God we, who were once enemies of God, can become his friends. The death of Jesus not only liberates humanity but also the whole of creation from its bondage to sin, death and satanic control (Colossians 1:19–23). In Jesus we are restored to doing once again what Jesus wanted us to do in the first place: to love the Lord with our whole being and our neighbour as ourselves.

A person is happy or blessed, according to the Bible, when they begin to respond to the mercy that God has revealed to us in his Son Jesus Christ. Further, a person is blessed when he aches for the coming of the Kingdom of God. A person is blessed when she begins to suffer pain and rejection because she refuses to serve false gods and decides to follow the crucified One.

The Bible also tells us that happiness lies more in giving than in receiving. The Old Testament people were commanded to return land to the landless one year in fifty and to cancel debts once every seven years. Jesus reinforced this teaching: 'Give, and it will be given to you. A good measure, pressed down, shaken together and running over, will be poured into your lap. For with the measure you use, it will be measured to you' (Lk 6:38).

In the biblical perspective, giving is not simply something we are commanded to do. We give and bless our neighbours because to give and to serve is to be in tune with the way God has structured this world. Those who are selfish and greedy will not be happy in this age and they will not inherit the earth in the age to come.

This concept of happiness radically confronts western secular views of well-being. Our consumer culture urges us to acquire huge numbers of material goods. The underlying assumption is that receiving is more sensible and practical than giving, and that we were made to live for comfort, pleasure and material satisfaction. Modern science strives to convince us that modern man can indeed live by bread alone – and by beer alone, by sex alone, by technology alone, by economic growth alone. But can he? When humans reject God and turn to false gods they lose the peace and blessedness that only God can bring. Good parts of creation become ugly and distorted. We can eat bread, drink beer, make love and make tools to the glory of God – or to the glory of idols. One way brings wisdom and life, the other can only bring death.

In this chapter we have examined four questions crucial to any philosophy of education. We have also attempted to suggest some possible implications for a Christian approach to the curriculum. Now we will turn our attention to the dominant secular perspective. How does it answer these questions?[8]

Notes

1. I have deliberately made a very long list of 'creatures'. I want to stress the variety of God's creation and to undermine particular theories of reality that reduce the world to such entities as mind and matter or physical 'stuff' and spiritual 'stuff'. To speak of the world in terms of matter and spirit (or just simply matter) is to misunderstand profoundly the structure of God's creation. In the Bible we encounter whole creatures, be they donkeys, lions, women, men or angels. These creatures display a host of irreducible dimensions or aspects such as size, weight, colour, volume, compassion, intelligence, trust etc. A genuine Christian understanding of reality needs to honour the richness, diversity and complexity of God's world.

2. There is good reason to believe that these laws about land-rest and debt-cancellation were obeyed – at least some of the time. In years of spiritual apostasy they were, of course, the first to be forgotten.

   During the life of Nehemiah there was a reformation and it is clear that these laws were obeyed. 'When the neighbouring peoples bring merchandise or grain to sell on the Sabbath, we will not buy from them on the Sabbath or on any other holy day. Every seventh year we will forgo working the land and will cancel all debts' (Neh 10:31).

   Jesus mentions these laws in the Lord's Prayer: 'Forgive us our debts, as we also have forgiven our debtors' (Mt

6:12). This passage certainly refers to forgiving sins but it also refers to this Old Testament law to wipe out financial debts that often cripple people. To ignore this is to 'spiritualise' a great deal of New Testament teaching.

3. It is fascinating to discover that there is an intimate connection between obedience to God's laws and 'signs and wonders' or miracles. For example, in Leviticus chapter 25 it is clear that God intended his people to rest the land eight years in fifty. There are seven years of Sabbath rest and the fiftieth year is referred to as the Year of Jubilee. In this year there is not only a year of rest for humans, land and animals but those Israelites who have lost their land are returned to their familial land. God explains very succinctly to Moses that obedient faith will guarantee sufficient food:

> Follow my decrees and be careful to obey my laws, and you will live safely in the land. Then the land will yield its fruit, and you will eat your fill and live there in safety. You may ask, 'What will we eat in the seventh year if we do not plant or harvest our crops?' *I will send you such a blessing in the sixth year that the land will yield enough for three years.* While you plant during the eighth year, you will eat from the old crop and will continue to eat from it until the harvest of the ninth year comes in. [my italics]

Leviticus 25:18–22

Nehemiah chapter 5 verse 11 indicates that the jubilee was obeyed in Nehemiah's lifetime.

4. All are equally valuable and mutually enriching. Rational knowing is only one way of apprehending. We can also speak of ethical, aesthetic, emotional, technical, agricultural and economic ways of knowing. All these kinds of knowing involve logical distinguishing, but they are not dominated by rational activity. At the same time, rational knowing should display ethical, aesthetic and responsible dimensions. Wisdom needs to pervade all these different types of knowing. Faithful theorising must be responsible,

motivated by an attitude of humble stewardship rather than mastery. Any view of knowledge that seems to be detached or impersonal leads to irresponsibility and scientific practice that is motivated by mastery not stewardship. (I am indebted to Hendrik Hart and Michael Polanyi for these comments on wisdom and knowing.)

5. Now, I am well aware that I am grossly oversimplifying at this juncture. There are many positions that could be termed secular or humanist that do not understand human beings as 'survival-machines'. By humanism I intend all those positions that construe man as autonomous in the sense that man is accountable only to himself. For example, I would describe Kant's worldview as 'humanistic' but this position would never understand a person to be simply a 'survival-machine'.

6. Loren Wilkinson, ed, *Earthkeeping: Christian Stewardship of Natural Resources* (Eerdmans: Grand Rapids, MI, 1980), p 209.

7. I owe this illustration of Adam and Eve developing simple tool-making to Richard Mouw.

8. I am indebted to Calvin Seerveld and Albert Wolters for many of the ideas in this chapter.

CHAPTER TWO

IDOLATRY, ENLIGHTENMENT AND THE SPIRIT OF CULTURE IN THE 1980s

In order to understand modern education and the textbooks that our children read, we need to grasp three important themes. First, we will explore what the Bible means by idolatry and then we will investigate the particular atheism and humanism of the eighteenth century. We will then turn our attention to the 1980s. The biblical theme of idolatry will help us to understand the spirit of the eighteenth century and this in turn will help us to understand our present decade.

1. Idolatry

A close study of Scripture will show that the prophets constantly reproached God's people because they had broken the eternal covenant, forgotten the Lord and begun to worship false gods and idols. Listen to Jeremiah, the great prophet:

> 'Cursed is the man who does not obey the terms of this covenant
> – the terms I commanded your forefathers when I brought them
> out of Egypt, out of the iron-smelting furnace.' I said, 'Obey me
> and do everything I command you, and you will be my people, and
> I will be your God. Then I will fulfil the oath I swore to your
> forefathers, to give them a land flowing with milk and honey' – the
> land you possess today.... There is a conspiracy among the people
> of Judah and those who live in Jerusalem. They have returned to

the sins of their forefathers, who refused to listen to my words. They have followed other gods to serve them. Both the house of Israel and the house of Judah have broken the covenant I made with their forefathers.

Jeremiah 11:3–10

In the Old Testament God established an agreement or a covenant with his people. He swore an oath to Abraham, Isaac and Jacob that he would give them and their descendents a paradise on earth, a land flowing with milk and honey. He promised to protect and love his people if they would only love and obey him. He commanded his people to obey all his wise laws. He wanted a people who would love each other, steward his world, show mercy to the poor and the foreigner, and love him, the King, with all their hearts and minds. As King, he had every right to expect human obedience. We have already seen that if the people of God had obeyed all these wise laws, the results would have been remarkable. No oppression. No broken marriages. No poverty. No unfaithfulness. God's healing presence and a faithful covenant people would have provided the perfect antidote to the ravages of sin, idolatry and satanic dominion.

But to walk with the Lord and obey his covenant required unusual trust. It demanded childlike faith in the promises of the Lord. For example, the people of Israel had to trust God to provide extra food during their holiday years. Remember for each fifty-year period the Lord had insisted that his people take eight years off. The land, the animals and the people had to have that rest.

The Lord also promised his people that if they obeyed him, he would fight their battles for them. 'Five of you will chase a hundred, and a hundred of you will chase ten thousand, and your enemies will fall by the sword before you' (Lev 26:8). Such promises from the great King demanded unbelievable faith. In Deuteronomy we read:

The officers shall say to the army: 'Has anyone built a new house and not dedicated it? Let him go home, or he may die in battle and someone else may dedicate it. Has anyone planted a vineyard and not begun to enjoy it? Let him go home, or he may die in battle and someone else enjoy it. Has anyone become pledged to a woman and not married her? Let him go home, or he may die in battle and someone else marry her.' Then the officers shall add, 'Is any man afraid or faint-hearted? Let him go home so that his brothers will not become disheartened too.'

Deuteronomy 20:5–8

It is quite clear from this passage that God preferred his people to have small armies. He wanted them to trust in his great power, not their own military might. Note the underlying implication that God longed for a people who would trust him in personal ways, but also in economic and political ones. A people who would expect their King to perform mighty deeds on their behalf. He did not want his people endlessly preoccupied with military matters and material prosperity, but rather to get on with the important task of living out his vision for them. God wanted his chosen people to show the surrounding pagan nations how to live *in every sphere of life*. He wanted justice, righteousness and abundant life to permeate the entire life of his people, and so he promised them that he would look after them faithfully if they got on with the job.

But if they disobeyed? This is surely one of the most painful aspects of the Bible. God promised his people food, wine, clothing, good health and complete protection from military defeat, famine, plague and wild beasts – if only they would trust him and obey his covenant! But God also promised them that he would bring a terrible judgement upon them if they disobeyed his covenant and embraced the worship of false gods and idols. Leviticus chapter 26 explains this in exhaustive detail. This theme recurs throughout the Bible. Take Ezekiel: 'For this is what the Sovereign Lord says: "How much worse will it be when I send against Jerusalem my four dreadful judgments – sword and famine and wild beasts and plague – to kill its men and their animals!"' (Ezekiel 14:21)

The Bible makes it emphatically clear that God is a holy God. He loves justice and righteousness and he hates iniquity. It is for this reason that it is crucial to follow the Lord and please him in everything we do. The prophets continually reminded the people of Israel that there are two ways you can go. You can either walk in a faithful covenant relationship with God or you can break covenant with him and turn to idolatry. There is no other possible path. It is impossible to find a neutral approach which allows you to avoid offending both the true God and false gods at the same time. You please either one and offend the other. That's it. But what precisely is idolatry? Surely modern people don't worship idols and false gods?

I want to argue that modern secular people do in fact worship false gods; they do practise idolatry and such idolatry brings a terrible curse. We've all heard the sermon where the preacher tells us that 'there's a cost in following Jesus' but few of us have heard sermons where we're told of the terrible cost that is involved in following idols. Listen to Moses:

> And God spoke all these words: 'I am the Lord your God, who brought you out of Egypt, out of the land of slavery. You shall have no other gods before me. You shall not make for yourself an idol in the form of anything in heaven above or on the earth beneath or in the waters below. You shall not bow down to them or worship them; for I, the Lord your God, am a jealous God, punishing the children for the sin of the fathers to the third and fourth generation of those who hate me, but showing love to thousands who love me and keep my commandments.'
>
> Exodus 20:1–6

To gain insight into these famous first two commandments, it is illuminating to consider the kind of pagan religion that confronted the people of God when they came into the promised land. The local Canaanite religion held that Baal and Asherah were the two most important gods to worship. Baal was the king and Asherah was the queen. They controlled the weather and a host of climactic features. They were, in short, fertility gods.

Believers and servants of Baal and Asherah were convinced that if they served them with dedication and commitment, Baal and his wife would make sure that the land would produce healthy crops and further that young women would bear many healthy children. Olives, grapes and wheat would abound as long as Baal and his celestial concubine enjoyed the worship of their followers. If one offended the gods, one could expect famine, plague and a host of other miseries. Baal was a god who had his own contract. He offered his followers a covenant in exactly the same way as God offered a covenant, but the contents of this covenant were completely different.

God expected his people to serve him – and only him. He wanted a people who were wise and obeyed his life-giving laws in all of life. Baal and Asherah were completely uninterested in their followers acting justly, loving mercy and walking humbly with their God (Mic 6:8). Their devotees believed that at the beginning of autumn the gods were forced, through extreme tiredness, to lie down and sleep for six months. We could say that they were hibernating gods.

The more intelligent followers of this ancient religion soon realised that Baal and Asherah urgently required an effective and reliable awakening at the beginning of spring in order that they could begin to fertilise the land. To accomplish this task, followers went to extraordinary lengths. Some of them engaged in loud ritual wailing for hour after hour, hoping to attract Baal's attention. Others slashed their wrists, arms and legs, producing a lot of blood which would hopefully entice the majestic couple out of bed. Further techniques were developed as time passed. Cultic prostitutes were hired to perform cultic sexual intercourse. When famine or plague threatened, children would sometimes be sacrificed to the gods.

Clearly this corrupt Canaanite religion offered its followers a completely different way of looking at the world from the vision of life that God had ordained. In the biblical view, God called his people to develop culture and civilisation (cities, music, scholarship, agriculture, commerce, etc) in obedience to his wise laws. The covenant people were called to develop the potential of creation to its fulfilment, but Baal religion had no interest or passion for this obedient and holy cultivation of the earth. The Baal worldview was exclusively concerned with the technique of 'proper ritual' and the propitiation of lustful gods; cultic prostitution and child sacrifice would satisfy the gods.

The religion of Baal not only provided an alternative vision of life to the biblical one, it also threatened to destroy that vision. Gradually the covenant people forgot the Lord's commission to cultivate the earth to the glory of God, and began to imitate the followers of Baal. This meant that the biblical vision slowly began to lose its distinctive and radical flavour, becoming more and more like a Canaanite religion. The people would say that they worshipped the Lord, the God of Abraham, Isaac, Jacob and Moses, but in time they transformed biblical religion into Canaanite obsession. Their religion was a form of 'syncretism': this simply means that two very different visions of life merge together. Paganism and biblical religion so fused that it became impossible to distinguish true religion from false!

There is an excellent example of 'syncretism' in Judges chapter 11. Jephthah is convinced that God will be pleased with him if he sacrifices his daughter to the Lord. This sad story reveals that Canaanite practices were gradually becoming commonplace among the covenant people. Syncretism is one of the major themes of the Book of Judges.

The Book of Hosea is of great interest with respect to syncretism. It shows us that cultic prostitution, wailing, slashing and child sacrifice had become so deeply embedded within the life of Israel that the vast majority of Israelites believed that they were commanded by the God of Abraham, Isaac and Jacob.

It is helpful to remember five aspects of Baal religion. First, it worshipped the created. Paul wrote:

> For although they knew God, they neither glorified him as God nor gave thanks to him, but their thinking became futile and their foolish hearts were darkened. Although they claimed to be wise, they became fools and exchanged the glory of the immortal God for images made to look like mortal man and birds and animals and reptiles.
>
> Therefore God gave them over in the sinful desires of their hearts to sexual impurity for the degrading of their bodies with one another. They exchanged the truth of God for a lie, and worshipped and served created things rather than the Creator – who is for ever praised. Amen.
>
> Romans 1:21–25

Baal religion focused upon the aspect of fertility in God's world and made it divine. It made part of creation its god. Baal religion invented false gods who somehow personified 'divine fertility'. These gods were Baal and Asherah.

Secondly, this pagan religion made idols or images of these gods. In the Book of Judges we read that

> Gideon built an altar to the Lord there and called it 'The Lord is Peace'. To this day it stands in Ophrah of the Abiezrites. That same night the Lord said to him, 'Take the second bull from your father's herd, the one seven years old. Tear down your father's altar to Baal and cut down the Asherah pole beside it.'
>
> Judges 6:24–25

Followers of Baal made poles or statues of their divinities. These idols or images were intended to represent the gods. Devotees of this pagan view realised that the idols were not the same thing as the gods; the idols merely imaged the gods.

Thirdly, we need to understand that Baal religion exchanged the beauty of God's covenant for a squalid and repulsive covenant; a covenant of manipulation, fear, cultic prostitution and child sacrifice.

Fourthly, idolatry and the worship of false gods takes away the wisdom and understanding that God's people are supposed to possess in abundance. The prophet Hosea explains:

> Hear the word of the Lord, you Israelites,
> because the Lord has a charge to bring
> against you who live in the land:
> 'There is no faithfulness, no love,
> no acknowledgement of God in the land.
> There is only cursing, lying and murder,
> stealing and adultery; they break all bounds,
> and bloodshed follows bloodshed.
> Because of this the land mourns, and all who
> live in it waste away; the beasts of the field
> and the birds of the air and the fish of the sea
> are dying.
> But let no man bring a charge,
> let no man accuse another,
> for your people are like those
> who bring charges against a priest.
> You stumble day and night,
> and the prophets stumble with you.
> So I will destroy your mother –
> my people are destroyed from lack of knowledge.
> Because you have rejected knowledge,
> I also reject you as my priests;
> because you have ignored the law of your God,
> I also will ignore your children.
> The more the priests increased,
> the more they sinned against me;
> they exchanged their Glory for something disgraceful.'
>
> Hosea 4:1–7

Wisdom and understanding fill peoples' lives when they understand God's covenant. A wise person will delight in justice, righteousness, faithfulness and compassion. He or she will expect God's faithfulness to covenantal obedience. Idolatry takes away this kind of wisdom because it exchanges God's wise laws for something disgraceful. It exchanges the true covenant for a false one. This passage also shows us that the very land itself experiences death and mourning. Why? Because idolatry brings a curse in its wake.

Fifthly, we need to see that idolatry dehumanises those people who practise it. Psalm 115 is most illuminating:

> Our God is in heaven;
> he does whatever pleases him.
> But their idols are silver and gold,
> made by the hands of men.
> They have mouths, but cannot speak,
> eyes, but they cannot see;
> they have ears, but cannot hear,
> noses, but they cannot smell;
> they have hands, but cannot feel,
> feet, but they cannot walk;
> nor can they utter a sound with their throats.
> Those who make them will be like them,
> and so will all who trust in them.
>
> Psalm 115:3–8

If a person serves a false god, he or she will become like the false god that person loves. Baal was pictured as a capricious, cruel, greedy and lustful god. Psalm 115 reveals to us that followers of Baal will be transformed into the image of Baal. God hates this because he wants men and women to image him. God wants a people who will live out his purposes for his creation.

Idolatry can take many forms. A modern example might help. It is possible to become so preoccupied with football and beer that a person can build his life around the game of football and the pub. This shows us how a person can focus upon the created and thus forget God and his call upon his life. Of course, it is possible to love the game of football and the drink we call beer in a way that is not idolatrous. Personally I love football and enjoy going to pubs. Idolatry creeps in when we distance ourselves from God and refuse to obey him in the way we integrate football and pubs into our lives as a whole.

It is also possible to worship the family. The family is a good part of God's good creation but it is possible to idolise it and depreciate the value of single people and the obedient stewardly response of the many other institutions of our modern world. It is easy for Christian political thinking to reduce its analysis of culture to the family and its complexity. A wise Christian political theory must strive to understand the stewardly callings of banks, business companies, sports clubs and governments as well as the family. (The Christian sociologist Tony Walter has made an important contribution to our understanding of 'family worship'. See bibliography.)

One of the key features of modern idolatry is that it does not usually involve communication with a deity or deities. Baal worship displayed a very obvious cultic component: singing, wailing and slashing. Secular idolatry often doesn't display a cultic aspect but it is idolatry nevertheless. This lack of cultic ceremony in secular religion can be explained by the simple fact that secular gods are less personal than Baal or Asherah. A person (or community) may worship football, the family, money, sex or power, but they do not usually sing or talk to these objects of worship.

Idolatry, at root, refuses to recognise God's rightful place as King of his creation. In idolatry human creatures focus upon the created and then they forget and ignore God. Idolatry is simply rebellion against the great King.

2. The Enlightenment

Now that we have some provisional grasp of idolatry, we can move on to explore the idolatry of the eighteenth century. Just as in Baal worship, our modern world practises idolatry. Many modern people reject God's covenant of mercy and turn to false gods and false covenants. All people either follow the true covenant (commanded ultimately by Jesus) or they follow a false covenant (commanded ultimately by Satan). It is easy to discern the false nature of Baal's covenant, but our modern world is not so simple. The eighteenth century has profoundly shaped our modern world and it will help us to have some grasp of this period.

The eighteenth century is often referred to as 'the Age of Enlightenment'. What exactly is Enlightenment? The great thinkers of this period were convinced that man had come of age. They believed that mankind could be liberated from ignorance, superstition and tradition. These thinkers believed that for thousands of years men had been bewitched by primitive beliefs and superstitions; men and women had lived in darkness, folly and utter ignorance. The world, according to these eighteenth century philosophers, was in bondage to unreason, stupidity and superstitious belief.

Ordinary people believed in ghosts, lucky charms, omens and the folly of chancing upon a black cat. Hidden spirits, foolish gods and capricious demons were simply everywhere. 'Cross my palm with silver, dearie, and I'll tell you your future. I see a handsome man approaching you!' Astrology, black magic, witches and souls floating into frogs; magpies that revealed the will of the gods; tarot cards that spoke of fate and untimely death. Paganism and Christianity, both Catholic and Protestant, had merged together. Simple folk would gaze ecstatically at a statue of the Virgin Mary, hoping their dedication would release their parents' burning souls from purgatory. The Inquisition demanded that people believed certain doctrines – on pain of violent death.

The syncretism, then, of paganism and a diluted Christianity provoked a deep contempt in the hearts and minds of those influential men and women in the eighteenth century who called for a new way.[1]

To be sure, the Reformation had called for a return to a much more authentically biblical Christianity. Without doubt, pockets of believers cried out to God for renewal and reformation. Christian communities were set up that proclaimed a new order, centred in Jesus Christ. But the great thinkers of the Enlightenment would not, could not, see this. The Reformation proclaimed that the antidote to superstition, folly and ignorance was the kingdom of Jesus Christ. This kingdom proclaimed an everlasting solution to the miseries of cruelty, sin and injustice: follow Christ and his new covenant. But the Reformation had slowly lost its burning zeal, its radical confrontation with idolatry. By the eighteenth century the Reformation had begun to wane. Its genius had collapsed into a solemn, dignified churchianity that knew no passion, no vision, no zeal, no suffering.

If Christianity had so merged with pagan vision; if the genius and beauty of biblical religion lay hidden, surrounded by confusion and unbelief, which way, which vision would grip the hearts and minds of men and women? Which covenant would disciple the nations? Whose promises would fire the imaginations, hopes and dreams of countless unborn shapers of our twentieth-century world? The Enlightenment proposed a new and daring vision – a vision of life, a way of seeing things that has had a powerful and lasting impact upon our modern world.

Basically, Enlightenment intellectuals had come to believe that the world was simply a huge piece of clockwork. A gigantic machine; a lump of matter – with no life. Humans were also machines but machines with a difference: they had powerful minds inside material bodies. Reality was no longer perceived as a rich, multi-faceted cosmos, created by a great and powerful God. Rather it was construed as a rather boring and predictable machine that functioned in a precise and determinate fashion. This grand machine, this dead matter, functioned by iron-clad laws of cause and effect. The world became a huge, disenchanted billiard table.[2]

Gripped by this view of the world, a new view of science and technology unfolded. If the world behaved in this predictable and mechanical fashion then science would reveal to mankind the precise workings of 'nature'. And if this were true, man could become the 'master and possessor of nature'. Science would provide complete knowledge of nature, and invention – or technology, as we call it today – would give mankind complete power over nature. This was the kernel of a new and aggressive vision. It was the dawn of a new and magnetic creed. It was, in fact, the beginning of a new idolatry.

Man stands alone and proud, mighty in power and wisdom, supremely equipped with reason and technology. He is lord and master of all he surveys. He is a being who claims autonomy – he is a law-unto-himself. Why should he fear God or gods? Belief and superstition, be it pagan or Christian must be rejected as primitive and unscientific. It is simply not rational.

Belief in the Resurrection? Impossible! Such events do not occur in our mechanical universe. The Lord God Science has revealed to us authoritatively that such putative incidents cannot occur. Belief in miracles? Ridiculous! Reason and science have revealed to us that miracles cannot transpire. God is a God of justice, righteousness and compassion? Absurd! Science has revealed to us that the world is mechanical and determined. It is foolish and naïve to believe in such fictions. Science investigates the brute facts. It is not concerned with purpose, meaning, justice or faith. That is mere subjective speculation and it has nothing to do with objective and scientific fact. The famous Scottish philosopher David Hume (1711–76) expresses this approach with great clarity:

> When we run over libraries, persuaded of these principles, what havoc must we make? If we take in our hand any volume; of divinity or school metaphysics, for instance; let us ask, Does it contain any abstract reasoning concerning quantity or number? No. Does it contain any experimental reasoning concerning matter of fact and existence? No. Commit it then to the flames: for it can contain nothing but sophistry and illusion.[3]

This passage confesses a new creed by which man shall live. It declares the deeply religious belief that reason, especially in the form of the scientific method, can provide exhaustive knowledge of the world of nature and mankind. This means that science becomes the source of all wisdom and all revelation. This creed advises us to trust the reliable word of the scientist. The scientist and the scientific community have deep insights into the true nature of reality and the laity (non-scientists) must trust this source of revelation.

Behind all this we can discern that Enlightenment intellectuals, just like the priests of Baal and Asherah, were completely rejecting the true covenant that God had proclaimed through his word: trust in me, obey my covenant, steward my world, unfold science and technology to my glory and I will bless you and protect you from all harm. Instead these intellectuals poured scorn upon the God of the covenant. Enlightenment men and women were, by and large, hostile to Christianity and the Scriptures.

It was as if they were saying to God, 'We can practise science and technology on our own, without you. We will unfold science and technology in our way, not your way. We have no time for your laws of justice, righteousness, mercy and faithfulness. We are masters and captains of our fate. This world belongs to us. We, and we alone, shall rule. We shall do whatever we like with your world. We will even destroy it if we please.'

And so was born a new creature. Humans who refused to follow the gods or God. A new and violent generation that would trust the power of reason and technique and that alone. Why did Enlightenment man turn his back upon both the God of the Bible and the many pagan gods he had served before? Why did he put his faith in the new secular gods of science and technology? What was in it for him?

To answer this difficult question we need to understand why twentieth-century people have become so infatuated with the power of science and the promise of technology. I believe the answer to this question is extraordinarily significant. All people, whether they call themselves religious or not, long for a state of peace and blessedness. We all experience pain, alienation and suffering; the curse of unfulfilled promises, sickness and haunting disappointments. We all know in our hearts that this world moans with pain and we long for a better land. All people long for what the Bible calls *shalom*: peace and justice soothing us and making their homes with us. The great promise of Scripture is that *shalom* is found in God alone. But not all men and women agree with this.

We have already discovered that the Baal religion believed that the good life would come if – and only if – people trusted Baal and obeyed his covenant of wailing and slashing. We know too from Scripture that the prophets lambasted Baal worship and clearly taught that Baal was a false god and that his covenant brought death. If you carefully investigate the writings of the Enlightenment thinkers you will discover that they too believed a creed. They tended to believe that all human misery, pain, hunger, violence and war could be completely eradicated if only humans would unleash the great powers of science and technology. Improvements in human understanding and mastery over nature would bring peace, wholeness and blessedness to the entire earth. Enlightenment thinkers often spoke of a future paradise that the fruits of science and technology would surely bring. Robert Owen, a prophet of the Enlightenment vision, speaks of the world to come:

> In this new world, the inhabitants will attain a state of existence, in which a spirit of charity and affection will pervade the whole human race; man will become spiritualized, and happy amidst a race of superior beings.
>
> The knowledge which he will thus acquire of himself and of nature, will induce and enable him, through his self-interest, or desire for happiness, to form such superior external arrangements as will place him within a terrestrial paradise.[4]

What will bring about such future bliss? The Enlightenment thinkers had only one answer: *progress in science and technology*. With sufficient increase in knowledge and control of nature, man would never die from hunger or disease. Material abundance would flow throughout the ends of the earth. Many Enlightenment intellectuals also believed that stealing, murder and all evil would come to an end as the fruits of scientific and technical progress would bring healing to the nations.

Progress would not only bring material abundance, it would also bring moral and spiritual perfection. Indeed, Owen even speaks of the power of progress to 'regenerate' people. Men and women would become, in time, perfectly moral, perfectly healthy and perfectly rational as the power of science and reason would shatter the forces of unreason, superstition and Christianity. The famous French thinker, the Marquis de Condorcet (1743–94), encapsulated this faith in progress and human genius in the following words:

> Such is the object of the work I have undertaken; the result of which will be to show, from reasoning and from facts, that no bounds have been fixed to the improvement of the human faculties; that the perfectibility of man is absolutely indefinite; that the progress of this perfectibility, henceforth above the control of every power that would impede it, has no other limit than the duration of the globe upon which nature has placed us.[5]

For such thinkers as Owen and Condorcet, man can perfect himself without God. Mankind does not need to be saved by Christ, he can save himself by the light of his reason and technical brilliance. Such eighteenth-century thinkers believed passionately that mankind could create his own heaven on earth by *trusting* in the human ability to understand and master his environment. This enterprise, this faith in progress, would solve all man's problems.[6]

As Christians we need to be discerning about this creed. Does it involve idolatry or is it acceptable to a follower of Jesus Christ? A little thought will convince us that idolatry is indeed inextricably interwoven with this vision.

The Enlightenment vision called men and women to trust not in Jesus Christ but in the human ability to control and master their environment. Mastery, not faithful stewardship, grips this approach to life. Man refuses to develop and unfold the earth to the glory of God but promotes himself to be king of the earth. This vision rejects God as rightful King and renders man a lawless despot of God's world. This is without doubt idolatry; man focuses upon his rational and technical powers and ignores the true King. God is rejected and man is crowned king.[7]

3. The 1980s

Now that we have some understanding of the Enlightenment we can turn to our modern world. Obviously a great deal has happened since the Enlightenment. Many people still believe in progress. A Chicago-based company produced a series of articles which clearly expresses this faith:

> Can we be sure that science and technology will find the answers? Can we be sure that solutions to our problems exist? No, but we can be sure that nothing but science and technology can find them, if they exist.... To put it as bluntly as possible: Science and technology must answer our problems. If they don't nothing else will.[8]

To understand 'nature' and to control her has exercised a profound spell upon our modern world. Magazine upon magazine conveys this kind of perspective. Advert after advert evangelises us with this gospel. Man has only to do scientific research and invent brilliant gadgetry and his problems will melt away. Philip Handler, President of the National Academy of Science (USA) tells us this:

> Our cultural malaise stems from a few bad experiences – from time-delay in meeting the high hopes and expectations raised in the minds of those who appreciate the great power of science, the force of technology. Those expectations have taken on a new light as science has also revealed *the true condition of man on earth*.... I retain my faith that the science that has revealed the most awesome and profound beauties we have yet beheld is also the principal tool that our civilization has developed to mitigate the condition of man.[9]

But modern man does not exude the same optimism as the

men and women of the Enlightenment. While many in the eighteenth century believed that progress in science and technology would bring a perfect world, few people believe that now. Utopia is not the dominant theme of the twentieth century.

What then is the prevailing spirit of this age? Modern children and adults seem more concerned with surviving than to rhapsodising about the future. Optimism has given way to pessimism. Each evening as we turn on our television sets we are reminded that wars, famine, disease, terrorism, pollution, misery, rape, meaningless work and a host of vicious problems plague our world. Yes, our children play with unbelievably sophisticated toys and our lives are made comfortable by every type of hi-tec gadget, and yet the promises of those Enlightenment evangelists seem empty, almost contemptible. Where is this man-made heaven-on-earth?

A darker side to science and technology is emerging day by day:

> Stinking rivers, filth in the air we breathe, omnipresent noise, the plunder of raw materials, weapons of devilish savagery – all these bear witness to the dark face of science and technology. Despite attempts by the experts to persuade us that such horrors are merely temporary problems thrown up in the course of progress, people have recently begun to rebel. The products and processes of science and technology are under sustained attack. Yet, seen on a broader canvas, there are even more serious allegations against science on a different level altogether. The crucial criticism – all the more potent because we are seldom consciously aware of the case that supports it – is the extent to which science dominates our lives, our 'worldview', habits of thought, human relationships, and values – our entire cradle-to-grave existence.[10]

In this dark and gloomy passage we can see something of the anxiety and pessimism that haunts the modern world. No longer do our intellectuals dream of future bliss. How can we with the memory of the Holocaust and Hiroshima, the threat of Chernobyl, the devastation of earthquakes, AIDS and the pointless violence of Heysel stadium?

Such comments are not restricted to a tiny number of alarmist bohemians. Many intellectuals and artists are beginning to convey a despairing pessimism about the human condition. R S Peters, perhaps the most famous British educational philosopher, wrote:

> Our basic predicament in life is to learn to live with its ultimate pointlessness. We are monotonously reminded that education must be for life; so obviously the most important dimension of education is that in which we learn to come to terms with the pointlessness of life.[11]

It is rather difficult to develop an exciting view of curriculum and education from this kind of philosophy. The famous English artist Francis Bacon shares Peters' conviction that life is ultimately pointless. Bacon has this to say about art:

> Also, man now realizes that he is an accident, that he is a completely futile being, that he has to play out the game without reason.... Man now can only attempt to beguile himself for a time, by prolonging his life – by buying a kind of immortality through the doctors. You see, painting has become – all art has become – a game by which man distracts himself. And you may say that it always has been like that, but now it's entirely a game. What is fascinating is that it's going to become much more difficult for the artist, because he must really deepen the game to be any good at all, so that he can make life a bit more exciting.[12]

Our age is gripped more by insecurity and despair than by hope. Life is painful and futile. Perhaps the 'great powers of science and technology' can mitigate our condition, but talk of utopia has lost its power to convert the masses. Survival and expediency are becoming the catchwords of our day. The 'great powers of science and technology' no longer promise us the promised land; they merely help us to survive and enjoy a little comfort.

How then does our modern secular culture answer our four questions? For many the world is a harsh jungle. Wisdom and knowledge are becoming increasingly synonymous with coping and survival. A person is simply a clever and adaptable animal, the product of chance, a survival-machine who has no intrinsic purpose or dignity. She seeks out some small pleasure, some anaesthetic; a few meaningless experiences of pleasure and consumption before death and the rotting of the body.

Recently, a well-known football manager commented that 'in football it's all a question of survival'. His words express the dominant spirit of the 1980s. Man struggles to survive in a harsh and hostile world. Unemployment, inappropriate skills, AIDS, acid rain, miserable, bad-tempered employers, earthquakes and drunken football fans threaten you. How do you survive? How do you cope? How do you adapt? How do you live safely in the land?[13]

As many people repent of their naïve faith in progress (things shall get better and better, there is no doubt), they turn to different gods. For some life is simply endless consumerism. 'Eat drink and be merry for tomorrow we die' might encapsulate this creed. An article in the *Guardian* conveys this well:

> Jason is a bit of a lad and he doesn't care who knows it. 'I know how to enjoy myself,' he says, 'and I don't mind spending some money to have a good time.' ... Jason and his girlfriend, Annette, believe in being taken out of themselves. They have their own sunbed installed in the spare bedroom of their flat in Wood Green, north London. Their skin is a uniform pale toffee colour. 'We're very careful about getting too much UVB,' says Annette. 'There's a lot of skin cancer about nowadays.' ... Before they discovered poppers and bombers, the couple found they would often sleep away most of the weekend. They had to leave the parties just as they were really getting going. Jason is a great believer in the work ethic, but it can be quite a strain. 'On Friday night, all I feel like doing is slumping in front of the telly,' he says. 'But if I gave into that I'd just be wasting my youth. I'd be living like an old man. A couple of bombers and I'm up on my feet again. What's wrong with that? You've got to live a bit, haven't you?'[14]

Perhaps it needs stressing that this article is no spoof. It is simply an article about a couple, Jason and Annette, who live in North London. Jason and Annette are coping and surviving; skin cancer might visit them but they're surviving. Perhaps life is futile but a few bombers will keep you going (until you die of a heart attack).

Lots of booze, loadsamoney, lots of bombers. How else do modern people cope and survive in a tough and painful world? Many find comfort and guidance in astrology, freemasonry, and contacting the dead; in a little bit of levitation or astral projection. Maybe some tarot cards as you sniff some coke. A culture that is saturated by survival, coping and money-making needs to find some spirituality that will provide a few kicks but not challenge unduly.

The Enlightenment boasted that the great powers of science and technology would abolish superstition. Ironically, it seems that these great powers have created such a meaningless materialism that superstition and pre-Enlightenment paganism threaten to dominate our post-Enlightenment world! A barren and spiritually exhausted humanism will always call into being a fascination with magic and the occult. Lives without meaning, purpose or integration will always seek spiritual satisfaction, either in Christ or the demonic. That is why many adults and children are turning away from simple atheism and materialism into the arms of astrology, levitation and contacting the dead. The false secular gods of scientific and technical progress no longer convince us; their promises have become hollow and jaded.

What impact does this mood of anxiety and pessimism have upon our children? They too experience the need to survive and cope in a harsh and hostile world. Survival is the name of the game. A bit of pleasure. A few kicks. For tomorrow may never come. A disaster might strike, and all the technical genius of mankind can do nothing to mitigate it. Many children experience deep-rooted anxiety and hopelessness. Where is hope in a world where it is very hard to find a meaningful job? Genuine joy is scarce; pain, loneliness and frustration are far more obvious.

Our secular world used to find comfort and hope in the Enlightenment's faith in progress. Man used to believe that he could live securely in the land by mastering his environment, by unleashing the power of his intellect and the force of his technical wizardry. But in the 1980s the very land itself threatens to dominate and to destroy man. It is as if the very creation itself writhes in agony, exhausted by human mastery and exploitation. Perhaps the very earth itself is beginning to 'vomit out' its idolatrous inhabitants (Leviticus 18:25)?

Could it be that Jesus Christ, the Creator and Redeemer of the world, is crying out to us in pain: 'Repent of your idolatrous trust in created things!'

> Turn to me and be saved,
> all you ends of the earth;
> for I am God, and there is no other.
>   Isaiah 45:22

Notes

1. I am aware that these brief comments about the syncretism of pagan religion and a diluted Christianity are oversimplified and cannot be applied right across the church up to the eighteenth century. However, just as Baal syncretism prevented the people of God from fully understanding their distinctive calling, so did the syncretism of pagan Greek philosophy with Christian doctrine in the medieval church. This philosophy had such an impact on the early church fathers and the medieval church that the biblical themes of creation, cultural mandate and obedient cultural formation were lost to the Christian church. Christianity became otherworldly and irrelevant. This emasculated Christianity called into

being the Enlightenment's preoccupation with mastery of the earth. Complete denial of the importance of the cultural mandate (Platonised Christianity) called into being a distortion of the cultural mandate in which mastery, not stewardship, predominated.

2. I would add that many eighteenth-century philosophers were torn between the view that all reality was machine-like (including man's mind) and the view that most of reality was machine-like (excepting human rational powers which were believed to transcend mechanical causation). Other views were developed as well. For the purposes of this book we need to notice the huge tensions that these views encouraged. For example, if the whole of reality is machine-like, then this would seem to rob man of his dignity as a creature who transcends the fixed and determined workings of 'nature'; humans become automatons who are not free and dignified but subject to fixed and determined natural laws. But if man is indeed privileged in his possession of a mighty and nature-transcending intellect, then one begins to wonder how man received this extraordinary organ. Herman Dooyeweerd has argued persuasively that a great deal of modern philosophy and thought has been plagued by this 'dialectical tension' (see bibliography for further details).

3. David Hume, *An Enquiry Concerning Human Understanding* as quoted in Locke, Berkeley, Hume, *The Empiricists* (Anchor Books: New York, 1974), p 430.

4. Robert Owen, *The Book of the New Moral World* (Effingham Wilson Royal Exchange: London, 1836), p xxi.

5. As quoted in Brayton Polka and Bernard Zelechow, eds *Readings in Western Civilisation* Vol 2 (Alfred Knopf: Toronto, Canada, 1970), p 165.

6. Whereas the medieval period tended to depreciate what I have called the cultural mandate (God's call to the human race to develop culture and civilisation to his glory), the

Enlightenment period tended to encourage the 'opening up' of many creational possibilities. For example, the medieval perspective tended to discourage technological innovation whereas the Enlightenment tended to encourage limitless and almost ruthless technological innovation. Both positions are distorted. But the Enlightenment did indeed open up scientific and technical possibilities. This is good and to be commended. However the dominant motif behind this exploration and development was autonomy and mastery. (See bibliography and in particular Goudzwaard's brilliant analysis of the Enlightenment in *Capitalism and Progress*.)

7. I am indebted to Bob Goudzwaard for many of the ideas in this section on the Enlightenment.

8. See R Middleton and B Walsh, *The Transforming Vision* (InterVarsity Press: Downers Grove, Ill, 1984), p 135.

9. P Handler, 'Edison Electric Institute Symposium' (supplement to *New York Review of Books* (27th September, 1979), p 15.

10. Quoted by Arie Leegwater, 'Creation: Does it Matter?' in *Life is Religion* (Paideia Press: St Catherine's, Ontario, Canada, 1981), p 249. Although the writer (B Dixon) conveys very well the impact of distorted and irresponsible science and technology, he does not seem to realise that it is not only 'in recent times' that people have rebelled against the products and processes of science and technology. For example, many nineteenth-century artists, philosophers and writers were deeply critical of science worship.

11. R S Peters, *London Educational Review* (Autumn 1973), p 1.

12. Quoted from J Russell, *Francis Bacon* (Methuen: London, 1965), p 1.

13. As I have intimated before it would be quite mistaken to claim that all humanists believe that humans are simply survival-machines, products of chance and natural selec-

tion. Many humanists would claim that people are rational/moral entities possessing enormous dignity. There are of course differences of opinion among humanists. But I think it is fair to say that there is a growing awareness among philosophers and intellectuals of a tension between a Darwinian view of reality and the view that claims 'privileged status' for reason and morality. Many 'pragmatising' and 'historicising' philosophers are acutely aware that historicism and Darwinism undermine the distinctiveness that our culture used to attribute to rationality and morality. Many teachers in comprehensive schools would like to hold to an 'optimistic' humanism that stresses rationality, dignity and morality; the difficulty and ambiguity of this position arises from the tension between a high view of rationality and a pragmatism and Darwinism that cannot make much sense of rationality and morality.

14. *The Guardian* (11th May 1988), p 16.

Part Two

The Textbooks

In the following chapters we will examine some of the many school textbooks that our children read. What basic worldview is being conveyed to them as they do their homework and prepare for their exams? Is it a biblical worldview or a humanistic one?

The 1988 Education Reform Act required all schools to provide a National Curriculum. It was introduced into schools in 1989. This National Curriculum consists of three 'core' subjects – English, mathematics and science, and seven foundation subjects – history, geography, technology, art, music, physical education and a modern language in a secondary school. In addition to these subjects schools are required to provide religious education as a part of the basic curriculum for all pupils. These proposals will bring a greater uniformity to schools, especially as there will be attainment targets for each core and foundation subject. These will establish what children will be expected to know and be able to do at the ages of seven, eleven, fourteen and sixteen. These attainment targets will be backed up by tests for children at these ages.

The way in which knowledge is likely to become even further fragmented into separate subjects, although useful for purposes of analysis, presents young people with a disjointed, often meaningless, view of the world. This tendency will be enhanced if no attempt is made to explain the interconnectedness and coherence of God's world. This separation of knowledge into rigid subject-areas goes against many of the recent attempts to integrate the curriculum. This is particularly evidenced in primary schools.

To facilitate our understanding of the curriculum and its content I propose to examine textbooks in the following subjects: science, maths, English, history, geography, technology, art and religious education. Of course there are literally thousands of textbooks presently used in schools and it would be mistaken to assume that they are all the same. But it is possible in this small survey to gain some understanding of typical textbooks. I also hope that my analysis will help parents to discern the underlying philosophies of the books their children read.

Before we begin I wish to point out that on the whole I am very critical of the textbooks we are about to examine. My general objection is that they tend to transmit a disenchanted and one-dimensional view of reality. At the same time I want to stress that in spite of this major flaw, many of them do contain all kinds of truths and insights. We all live in God's world and we are all forced to give some account of the order that this world displays. Even if a theory is developed in the light of a distorted and impoverished view of reality, it is possible to learn a great deal about God's world from that theory.[1]

I realise that I am dealing with many difficult and complicated issues in this chapter, but for the sake of identification and analysis, it has been necessary to simplify some of them and generalise.

CHAPTER THREE

SCIENCE

Let's begin with a biology textbook. The following passage is from *Science for Life*:

> Earth is the only planet known to have life on it... It is thought that under these conditions simple organic molecules were formed from the atmospheric gases and these were brought down to the surface by the heavy rains. Here they collected in seas and lakes to form what has been called the primeval soup.
>
> The primeval soup was made up of the organic molecules dissolved in water. It is thought that some of these molecules combined to form the basic building blocks of life – amino acids and nucleic acids. These combined at random until millions of years later they had become simple forms of life that were capable of reproducing themselves by dividing and growing.... The first recognisable animals were found on the Earth about 600 million years ago.... Plants and animals have since changed, or evolved, in different ways into the forms we see today.... In 1861 Charles Darwin suggested that natural selection was the basis of evolution. Darwin noticed that animals and plant are never exactly the same, they show variation. He realised that all living things are struggling to survive. Darwin concluded that those animals or plants that survived to breed would be those whose variations best suited them to their environment.[2]

This passage conveys to us a particular view of the world. In this view all living things are struggling to survive. All living things have come from the primeval soup. Successful adapta-

73

tion seems to be the dominant thrust of all change and all life.

What kind of world is being presented to young people? On the surface it seems to be a rather arid, colourless and uninviting world. Chance and successful adaptation appear to be the key concepts. Creatures do not play and dance before the King; they struggle to survive. A creature's environment continually threatens its 'future prospects'. Chance may deal you a fine hand; or it may deal you a bad one. Who can say when natural selection will strike?

What view of wisdom or knowledge does this passage imply? It is very difficult to generate any view of knowledge or rationality merely from the concepts of chance and survival-value. Rationality, at least in its normal usage, demands a coherent account of order and lawfulness that this Darwinian perspective seems unable to develop. (By Darwinism I mean a particular theory of evolution which stresses gradual change, chance and natural selection. Many competing evolutionary theories reject these assumptions. For example, there are Marxist, 'punctuated equilibrium', theistic and Lamarckian evolutionary alternatives to orthodox Darwinism. It also needs to be stressed that many secular biologists are now deeply critical of New-Darwinian orthodoxy. For instance, see *The Great Evolution Mystery* by Gordon Rattray Taylor [Abacus: London, 1984].) In this view, then, knowledge must be understood as a rather sophisticated survival mechanism; people are disposed to 'know' certain things because this will help them survive.

What view of a human being does this passage convey? It seems clear that 'all living things are struggling to survive', including men, women and children. A human being might be described as a 'survival-machine'. He is constantly adapting to his environment, hoping desperately that he will survive. Our primitive ancestors struggled against the onslaughts of sabre-toothed tigers and ferocious wolves by developing appropriate weaponry. Modern people do not deal with such hostilities but they are forced to adapt in the face of unemployment, new technology and acid rain.

This theme of adaptation to one's environment is brought out well in the science textbook *Scientific Eye*:

> Two hundred years ago no one could have guessed that the black moths might take over Birmingham. No one can now guess what will make **you** fittest for the life ahead.
>
> Look around the class. All the children are different. Some have curly hair. Some have blue eyes. Some have brown skin. Some can run fast. Some can scream loudly.
>
> At school the best things to be good at are probably exams, whispering, and not annoying teachers. The colour of your hair, your eyes, and your skin doesn't matter much.[3]

This passage is most revealing in that the theme of fitness is extended into the lives of children. Good behaviour is preferable because it will increase one's ability to survive. Such 'evolutionary ethics' can lead to the conclusion that weak and handicapped people should be eliminated because such action will increase the survival prospects of stronger humans.

What view of happiness does this perspective encourage? Will we be happy if we love our enemies? Probably not. It would seem more advisable to get rid of them. Natural selection will probably not reward the virtuous, and the blessed will be those who get the boot in – early! Natural selection is rather unconcerned with ethical choice; she is too busy eliminating the botched and the bungled, the weak and the powerless.

A number of things can be said about this Darwinian view, but I will restrict myself to the following. Many people, Christian and non-Christian, feel uncomfortable with this view of the world. Some Marxists would argue that this understanding of biology is repulsive because it develops a view of evolution which seems to ignore key Marxist concepts such as 're-volution' and 'co-operation'. Marxist biologists prefer to explain evolution in terms of co-operation, and by doing this they reject the Darwinian account which seems to stress competition and survival-value. Further, many Marxists reject the Darwinian assumption that the process of evolution is very slow and gradual; they prefer to extend their concept of 're-volution' into evolutionary change. They embrace a view of evolution in which species change very quickly and violently into higher life-forms.

Many other approaches to life and reality, apart from Christianity and Marxism, reject this extreme form of Dar-winism. Many people believe that human beings are noble and fine creatures because they possess the faculty of reason and this sets them apart from the 'beasts'. In this view reason is stressed; chance is not so important. Some philosophers have developed views of evolution in which a rational force dominates the process. But Darwinism, in its most developed form, radically undermines this approach. Chance, not reason governs the universe.[4]

Many thinkers are also devising creationist alternatives to the many competing evolutionary perspectives on offer. Here again there is great variety and diversity. (By creationism I simply mean theories of human origins that reject evolutio-nary theory.)

When we begin to investigate biology in terms of the many different ways that people look at the world, we begin to realise that it is possible to develop theories that arise out of different views of the world. It is possible to develop, at the very least, Darwinian, Marxist, and Christian meaning-frameworks for biology. Each position will tend to develop different accounts of biological structure and meaning.

Let's now look at some more biology.

The human body is a living machine made up of organ systems. These organ systems link up and work together to keep us alive. An example of one of our organ systems is the respiratory system – made up of the nose, mouth, windpipe and lungs.[5]

In this passage from *Science for Life* a mechanistic approach to life is being assumed. People are simply presented as if they were clever and sophisticated machines. Is this simply a neut-ral and 'value-free' perspective that we are being offered? I don't think so.

The biblical perspective is quite different. A person is a religious creature who stands before the face of God. Unlike a clock or a video-tape machine, a person is God's image-bearer and he or she responds to God from his or her heart. A person does indeed manifest physical and chemical properties. We all have a certain size and weight, and there is without doubt a chemical aspect to the brain. But human beings manifest many other kinds of properties. We hope, pray, love, scheme, imagine, play and feel. In that sense we are different kinds of creatures from rocks, plants or animals. We could even say that God has created (at least) five different kinds of creature. There are angels, humans, animals, plants and non-living creatures, such as copper and iron. Each kind of creature has its own kind of created glory; it is important not to confuse them.

In my view it is misleading to understand a person as either a composite of mind and matter or even a composite of body and soul. Biblical anthropology always focuses upon the whole person. Our hope is in the resurrection of the body in the context of the renewed creation. We do not hope to be immaterial souls dwelling in heaven. This means that a biblical anthropology must distinguish between the entire person and the many different properties that human beings display. (More precisely we could say that heaven is our glorious waiting-room and the renewed earth is our final destination.)

Our passage in *Science for Life* tends to eliminate these crucial creational differences and treats the human body as if it were a machine. In actual fact the implicit view of the world here tends to assume that all objects in the world can be understood as machine-like. This has quite crucial implications for the normal way that sex is taught in our schools. Let's move on now to a typical treatment of sex:

> Men and women experience sexual tension. This is sometimes called the sex drive, and is perfectly normal. Married couples usually release this tension by having sexual intercourse. This usually finishes with a climax or orgasm. In men, the climax comes when the sperm are ejaculated from the penis. In women, the orgasm is

harder to describe, and some women never have one. This is quite normal and sexual intercourse can be just as satisfying without an orgasm.

Stimulating one's own sexual organs to release tension and give sexual pleasure is called masturbation.... In men, the tip of the penis is the most sensitive area of the sexual organs. If this is stimulated by rubbing, the penis will become erect. Further stimulation, during masturbation or sexual intercourse, will lead to the ejaculation of sperms and the male orgasm.[6]

Here we have a seemingly factual and 'objective' approach to sex. This textbook has told us that the human is a machine and now we are given a mechanical description of a person's sex organs. The entire account attempts to give us value-free information about sex. Does it succeed?

It seems to me that this is a very *minimalistic* approach to sex. What do I mean by that? Certain aspects of sex are considered in great detail (the physical, chemical and biological aspects in particular) but there are many aspects to sex that are completely forgotten. Let's describe the sexual act in terms of a richer, more biblical perspective.

When a man and a woman make love we can distinguish two people who are involved. Their bodies are shaped in different ways. They move together as they make love. Their bodies press tightly together; their hearts beat harder as the excitement grows. The man and the woman tell each other how much they love each other. There is deep trust between the couple; they have both entered in to a covenant of marriage. They laugh and joke together as they relax together. This couple do not view each other as objects of consumption but delight in each other. Their marriage has passed through difficult times but they have remained faithful to each other.

In this description of sex we are trying to honour all the good aspects of the sexual act. All the aspects are equally real and important. This contrasts quite strikingly with our textbook. It seems that only the physical, chemical, biological and 'pleasure' aspects of sex are real. Why is this? I believe it is because a materialistic philosophy or worldview is being tacitly assumed. The world is considered to be matter in motion and so a minimalist analysis of sex ensues.

What is the impact of such an approach to sex upon children? Quite simply, such a perspective tends to brutalise and deaden them to the true nature of sexual intercourse. From a Christian perspective, sex is a beautiful and fascinating gift from God. Sexual activity, just like any other human activity, needs to respond to God's intentions and ways. Healthy sexuality brings great joy to men and women but distorted sex brings a great deal of misery and pain.

We live in a culture that has distorted many of God's gifts. Just as technology can be developed in sinful ways, sexuality can also be twisted and distorted. Such painful sexual distortions as rape and marital infidelity bring unbelievable torment into many people's lives. If you spend time speaking with men or women whose spouses have betrayed them, you begin to understand this kind of misery. God gives us his laws and ways because he does not want us to suffer these haunting afflictions.

A wise sex education will help children to understand the many rich facets of sexuality. Such dimensions as commitment, trust, love, playfulness, friendship, imagination, technique, and responsibility should never be stolen from such instruction. Of course, in biology we focus upon the biological aspect of reality; we attempt to understand the peculiar biological structure of sexuality but such needed abstraction must always be mindful of the wholeness of sex. A Christian approach to sex education will never be reductionistic. This simply means that we will refuse to reduce the true meaning of sexuality to the physical, chemical, biological and 'pleasure' aspects. These aspects are real aspects of sexuality but there are many others as well. All are good and important; all fit together and, like a jigsaw puzzle, need each other.

Before we turn to a different topic we need to probe just one more point. On page 100 of *Science for Life* the issue of abortion is raised. We are told this:

> An abortion is a deliberate miscarriage. There are many reasons
> for having an abortion, some of which are considered acceptable
> and others which are not.[7]

What is going on here? It seems apparent that a certain
authority is being appealed to. Human society might deem
some practices acceptable and other practices unacceptable.
Abortion, in this view, might be considered acceptable in one
decade and unacceptable in another. But precisely *who*
decides what is right or wrong remains ambiguous. Is it the
government, 'the will of the people', the medical profession
or the prevailing fashion? Whatever the answer may be,
human beings are assumed to be autonomous (self-govern-
ing). Man is not accountable to God or the gods; neither is he
accountable to an impersonal moral order. Somehow he
decides what is right or wrong.

Now it may be argued that this particular passage on abortion does not explicitly affirm the supreme authority of
'human consensus' or a particular institution such as the 'government' or 'the medical profession'. But the passage does
seem to suggest that if there is any say in the matter it is a
human say that counts. The possibility that there is a God to
whom we are responsible is simply discounted as not worthy
of serious consideration.

What, then, is the overall message of this particular biology
textbook? First, we are presented with a Darwinian view of
human and non-human origins that seems to stress chance and
natural selection. A mystical power (natural selection) brings
forth an extremely complicated and ordered world of
humans, animals, plants and non-living stuff. There is no
mention at all that to believe in the great power of natural
selection requires great faith. Somehow one particular
perspective on human origins is presented to us as dogma that
has become certain knowledge. What about those who cannot
generate sufficient faith in this particular god or power
(natural selection)? There are many who cannot believe in

this powerful and impersonal force; it requires too much faith!

Secondly, a view of personhood is developed in which mechanical metaphors are continually invoked. A person seems to be a rather clever and sophisticated machine – a machine that must strive to survive; a machine that must adapt in the face of a bleak and merciless environment.

Thirdly, a perspective on sex is developed which focuses exclusive attention upon the physical, chemical, biological and pleasure aspects of sex. Crucial aspects of sexuality are ignored.

Fourthly, questions of right and wrong seem to be referred to 'human consensus'. The human community is the ultimate judge of such matters. In ultimate terms ethical decisions mean little in a universe of chance and natural selection.

In conclusion we would do well to understand that this particular treatment of biology indoctrinates children into a mechanistic, Darwinian worldview. It is all the more disturbing that this particular worldview is simply presented as 'fact'. And we all know that you can't argue with the facts! Children are not only being indoctrinated into a mechanistic worldview, they are also prevented from grasping crucial biblical themes. We could say that children are being deadened to the biblical worldview.[8]

Notes

1. I am referring here to the concept of common grace. I want to make it very clear that people with secular or pagan worldviews have a great deal to *teach Christians*. One can learn a tremendous amount from Marxists and such movements as 'Greenpeace'. Sadly, Christians have tended to *abnegate* their distinctive calling in such areas as scholarship, engineering, business, banking, politics, town-planning and art. This means that they often do not know how to relate their faith to our highly complicated

world and may well end up embracing the dominant secular perspectives. In politics, for example, one comes across Christians who 'Christianise' conservatism, socialism, liberalism, communism, fascism and green politics.

To realise this is to become at once both very sad and very hopeful. Christians are beginning to realise that God claims all of life and there is a real desire to develop this belief. A major obstacle to this endeavour is this: how do we sensitively learn from secular and pagan perspectives and at the same time distance ourselves from these perspectives? This is a very complicated issue and there is no space here to develop my few brief comments.

The answer to this question lies in the very nature of idolatry. If we accept that God's world is immensely rich and displays many different dimensions which are structured and ordered by his word, it is very easy to 'absolutise' or worship one or two of these aspects and thus base one's life around a distorted view. But even in this distortion one will unlock all kinds of secrets and mysteries about God's world – even if the 'meaning-framework' presupposed is very inadequate. For example, in my view, the mechanistic way of understanding the world is profoundly mistaken. But many scientists and engineers who have 'soaked in' this perspective discover and have discovered all kinds of possibilities and insights.

2. Keith Bishop, *Science for Life* (Collins: London, 1984), pp 14–15.

3. Adam Hart-Davis, *Scientific Eye* (Bell and Hyman: London, 1985), p 54.

4. Darwinism always threatens to undermine the position that rationality transcends survival-value or natural selection. To put it crudely, a more old-fashioned humanism preferred to locate rationality above 'nature'. This means that the dignity and worth of each human person is derived from his rational/moral nature. Kant upheld this

view. Darwinism undermines this position by insisting that a person's rationality can be understood in terms of 'natural selection' and survival-value. Rationality is not the divine in us; it is simply a word that refers to human inferential stratagems (ways of thinking) that help us to survive.

5. Keith Bishop, *op cit,* p 54.
6. *Ibid*, p 95.
7. *Ibid*, p 100.
8. In this section on biology I have argued that facts and theories are never neutral. I would now like to present this position in a more technical fashion.

What we take to be a 'fact' is deeply coloured by our theories; observation is always theory-laden. At the same time a particular theory always takes shape and form in the context of a particular paradigm or research programme. A particular paradigm will largely determine what is believed to be an 'observation statement'. There is no such thing as 'immaculate perception'. This is a familiar theme in recent philosophy of science. Philosophers, such as Kuhn, Lakatos, Polanyi, Feyerabend, Putnam, Dooyeweerd and many others have presented powerful arguments for this position.

The story does not end there. A given paradigm is intimately connected to 'ontological' commitments. Philosophical theories of reality (materialism, idealism, Cartesian dualism, Aristotelian hylomorphism, etc) betray our worldview commitments. Such theories articulate at a theoretical level how we understand or slice up reality. These ontological theories are accordingly rooted in our ultimate or religious commitments. So if a person or community believes that (something called) matter is self-existent (divine), then this religious belief will control what a person takes to be 'the facts'. Richard Russell and Arthur Jones have developed the following diagram to illuminate this 'hierarchy of commitments'.

THE HIERARCHY OF COMMITMENTS

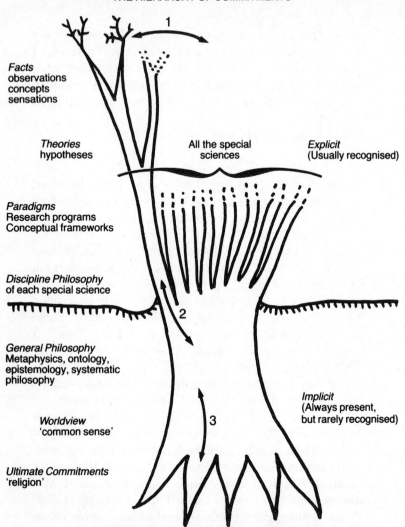

Facts
observations
concepts
sensations

Theories
hypotheses

All the special
sciences

Explicit
(Usually recognised)

Paradigms
Research programs
Conceptual frameworks

Discipline Philosophy
of each special science

General Philosophy
Metaphysics, ontology,
epistemology, systematic
philosophy

Implicit
(Always present,
but rarely recognised)

Worldview
'common sense'

Ultimate Commitments
'religion'

Notes: (1) It is not true, either in fact or in principle, that the special sciences
are autonomous with respect to each other (1), to philosophy (2), or
to religion (3).
(2) There is no simple relationship between religion and the content of
a special science. The influence is both real and decisive, but
operates through a hierarchy of commitments which must be
'dug out'.
(3) The development of self-critical Christian philosophy is mandatory.
Otherwise pagan commitments will reign at all levels.

The Bush of Human Knowledge (Dr Arthur Jones)
Figure 1

CHAPTER FOUR

ENGLISH

All kinds of stories, plays, poems and articles are used as basic texts in the teaching of English. What kind of worldview is being transmitted to our children as they read such literature? I have selected three pieces of writing that will give us some idea.

The first piece deals with a group of people and their conflicting views of life. The second piece offers us an interpretation of modern technology and its impact upon the world. The third piece concerns a 'ghost story'. Let's turn to our first piece.

In the textbook *English Workshop, Vol 3* there is a very interesting chapter called 'The People we are'. It begins like this:

What makes us what we are?

The people at Linda's Christening have each got a different answer. Between them they give the usual answers to this question, though no-one has yet proved that any one of them is more correct than the others.

What do you think?

The following suggestions could form an agenda for a discussion or just be used to help you sort out your thoughts. Keep a note of your answers and ideas. They'll be useful for any work on this subject you do later on.

Parents
Money
School
Personality
Luck
Surroundings

These are usually considered to be the major influences on our lives.[1]

We are then given a picture of Linda's Christening. Different people express their views via 'bubbles'. In the scene we have a priest, who has just christened Linda. He is surrounded by the parents of the child, the grandparents and a few friends; he does not seem to have a view. Five different people express their views of life. Bernie believes that luck and good contacts will bring the good life. Marge's mum believes that plenty of love will see Roger and Marge through (in spite of insufficient funds). Roger seems to believe that 'getting the right place' might help. Roger's dad seems to believe that good schooling and getting a good job should be the focus of Linda's life. Mr Jones believes that Linda will have 'to stand on her own two feet'; coping with a tough world will straighten her out.

The child reading this book is presented with a scene from a church where the vicar doesn't really have a view, and five other people express five different views of the world that convey conflicting commitments: money, luck, good contacts, comfortable homes, schools that will help you get a decent job and stand on your own two feet. These issues, it is true, dominate the lives of most British people. But they indicate, at heart, a way of life that is hollow and tame, devoid of any serious wrestling with life, simply accepting things as they are. These five different approaches to life are, at root, idolatrous ways of living.

We have seen that the Bible understands an idolatrous way of living as exchanging the truth for a lie. Instead of focusing upon God and walking in his ways of stewardship, justice, righteousness and faithfulness, we focus upon something created and put our trust in it, forgetting God and his claims upon our lives. When we do this we are unable to live in this world as God intends us to live. Idolatry always creeps into our lives when we distance ourselves from him and forget him:

> 'I will punish her for the days
> she burned incense to the Baals;
> she decked herself with rings and jewellery,
> and went after her lovers,
> but me she forgot,' declares the Lord
>
> Hosea 2:13

This theme of serving false gods and forgetting the Lord was a constant cry of the prophets long ago. But modern people must heed it, too. The idols that confront us in contemporary Britain are not Baal, Molech, Chemosh or Asherah. They are actually much more subtle and respectable: Economic Growth (at any cost), Science as Revelation, and Technology as Power have become the great idols of our culture. But people also believe in 'luck', 'destiny' and 'the stars'. Jesus speaks of 'money' as a possible object of worship (Luke 16:13), and the prophet Habakkuk speaks of 'power' as a false god (Habakkuk 1:11). We live in a highly complicated modern world where there are plenty of false gods on offer.

What then do we really discover in the seemingly happy scene described in the English textbook? People living out their lives in obedience to false gods, and the representative of the Christian church, happily baptising a baby girl, quite unconcerned by such idolatry. Such a picture of this conforming priest can only activate in children a profound contempt for Christianity. If Christianity is reduced to a cultic affair – christenings, confirmation, marriage and funerals – the light and healing power of the gospel is never allowed to touch most aspects of life. The beauty and glory of Christianity is simply never expressed; it is hidden to both children and adults.

I would add at this point that Christians themselves, whether evangelical, liberal or Roman Catholic, have encouraged the view that the biblical perspective has little to say about most of what we call life. Biblical religion stresses that all the many different spheres of human life, be they business, banking, town-planning, sport, art, scholarship etc, can be redeemed. It does not speak of sacred and secular areas of life. It simply speaks of covenantal obedience and covenantal disobedience. This obedience cuts through all of these areas. This problem, often called the problem of dualism, is discussed very fruitfully in *The Transforming Vision* (see bibliography).

It would almost seem that this scene in a church reinforces our culture's deepest prejudices. Man is simply a survival-machine, a clever and resourceful animal who has managed to cope in this hostile world by pitting his wits against 'nature'. So far he has managed, but he must be ever vigilant. Death and disease threaten, and life is harsh. Man is alone and lonely; the universe is gigantic and without meaning. There is no God to comfort and protect this clever animal. He must survive in this world by the light of his reason and technical ability. God and the gods are dead. This might be the creed of any one of the people present in this scene.

The biblical view of man, the image and glory of God, is simply not entertained. Biblical themes, such as prayer, atonement, sin, creation, stewardship, miracles, shalom, wholeness, integration, purpose and joy do not crop up. Such a perspective is not even presented and then rejected. It is not deemed worthy of serious consideration. Christianity is merely a cultic performance that we exploit at birth, marriage and death.

As Christians we need to understand just how bankrupt so much modern education has become. If a child's horizon of happiness is focused upon chance, luck, coping and struggling alone in a harsh cosmos, we should not be surprised when children behave so poorly and seem so dissatisfied with life. If we give young people stones when we should be giving them bread, they will not thank us.

Recently there has been much talk in the media about 'lager-louts' and increasing crime among the young. These phenomena need to be related to questions of worldview. I would surmise that 'surprised' parents often feel nurtured by a more optimistic humanism that speaks of 'progress', 'dignity' and 'reasonableness'. In this view dignity and respect are stressed. But younger people do not tend to share this commitment. 'Hope, dignity and progress' do not activate a great response in most young people. A great deal of education, it seems to me, oscillates between these two poles of humanism. At one moment a teacher might speak of the tremendous worth and dignity of children and then ten minutes later will convey the view that life is really meaningless – you've got to cope and nobody can be right or wrong.

If life is ultimately pointless, then education becomes a procedure we go through in order to survive and cope. Of course there are many people with a humanistic worldview who do not believe that life is meaningless. As I have intimated before, many thinkers and shapers of our modern culture understand people as dignified and rational creatures. This philosophy, which stresses rationality, progress and ethics and is best exemplified by the philosopher Kant, is vibrantly opposed to a view of life that stresses survival and coping. But the spirit of our time is turning away from this more optimistic humanism. The spirit of the 1980s and the dominant spirit of our schools is much more pessimistic and pragmatic. It seems to me that a central theme in many schools' understanding of life can be called 'Industrial Darwinism'. Children must be prepared for their industrial and entrepreneurial future and little else can be said. Progress? Sweet reasonableness? Morality? Nice ideals but let's get on with the important task of becoming and remaining wealthy. What a contrast to the biblical framework which speaks of God's call to steward his world fruitfully. This approach is positively saturated with meaning, surprise and promise; even the most humdrum human task becomes pregnant with purpose.

Writing a play, poem, sketch or story, as part of an English lesson becomes a meaningful activity when practised within a Christian meaning-framework that stresses the importance of creation and stewardship. God loves imaginative, subtle, inventive and witty language. He loves to watch children and adults exploring language and imagination. The Lord delights in all these rich and deft touches he has put into drama and story-telling. We and our children are called by the Lord to celebrate these good gifts.

We do not teach a child to read and write simply because it will help him or her to get a job. We encourage a child to savour language, to play with language, to rejoice with language, simply because human beings image the Lord and we are called to serve and preserve the earth. We could say that poetry and story-writing, for example, reveal to us one of the many possible ways of developing and unfolding God's creation. Let's listen to Scripture:

> Who let the wild donkey go free?
> Who untied his ropes?
> I gave him the wasteland as his home,
> the salt flats as his habitat.
> He laughs at the commotion in the town;
> he does not hear a driver's shout.
> He ranges the hills for his pasture
> and searches for any green thing.
>
> Job 39:5–8

The Lord God gave the donkey the wasteland as his home. But how does the Bible reveal this to us? Through poetry. These words and rhythms make us sensitive to the enchantment of reality.

The article below is used in a textbook as an exercise in comprehension. The pupil reads the article carefully and then answers about fifteen questions.

I was listening sleepily to that ingenious contraption, my digital clock radio, the other morning, when I half-heard one of those items that infects your day. It was about a new invention. A genius has decided that we wait too long at supermarket check-outs, and so he has developed a considerate computer to let the brain take the strain. It all involves weighing, and tearing off special little tags from each item you buy, and feeding them into a machine and weighing again.

Now I can recall a time when there were few long queues in supermarkets, because the companies ploughed their profits into employing two people at each check-out: one to ring up and the other to help you speedily pack. Remember? It was also when every garage was staffed by friendly men who filled the car up, checked the oil and even did the tyres, before an infernal machine encased a solitary soul in glass by the till, reading off the digits and charging you accordingly. It meant jobs for them; and for you... people who had the time to be jolly, grouchy, helpful or saucy.

Maybe you believe in that sort of progress. But I would like to smash the dreadful machines....

The computer generation (God help them) assumes that it is better to calculate, buy petrol, tell the time, work out your holiday plans, pay your bills, and even shop, with the aid of a computer. After all, our civilization is founded, now, on the certainty that we can kill by remote control, and a computer error could unleash Armageddon. The age of the computer is the age of dehumanisation.[2]

This piece of writing actually presents children with a false dilemma. A dilemma can be defined as 'an argument in which a choice of alternatives is presented, each of which is fatal'. It is a device for coaxing people into looking at the world in our way, and also blinding them to possible ways of thinking and acting that our dilemma refuses to acknowledge.

This article does precisely that. It reveals a squabble between two poles of modern humanism. We have already seen that many modern people have been eager to embrace the gospel of Progress. Many have believed passionately in the promise of reason and technical mastery to bring in the promised land. But not everybody trusts this way.

They look at the rivers and they see dying fish; they look at the forests and they see dead trees; they look at the many tedious and dehumanising jobs that people do. They look at the proliferation of sophisticated killing machines and the murder that grips the hearts of many humans, blinded by visions of future bliss that justify the most outrageous crimes. And they begin to doubt. They begin to wonder. Perhaps their faith in progress, science and technology is a misplaced faith. Perhaps these gods do not deliver the goods. Perhaps we have been besotted with a grand illusion.

Such people abandon faith in progress. But where do they go?

To help us understand their dilemma, I offer the following thoughts. Some people today believe that science, technology and endless material consumption are the *angels of light* that will deliver us from all misery and pain. They may or may not believe in the possibility of a perfect future. But they do believe that if there are any solutions to the world's problems then they reside in progress in science and technology. All other ways are illusory.

However, many others reject this faith. For them, progress itself is the problem. Machines are the problem. Technical innovation is the problem. Computers are evil. All technology should be abolished. In this approach science and technology are the *demons of darkness* that threaten our very existence.

It is at this point that wisdom, discernment and a biblical perspective are urgently needed.

Are we for or against football? Are we for or against trees? Are we for or against mountains? Are we for or against animals? Are we for or against humour? Are we for or against music? Are we for or against windows? Are we for or against paintings? Are we for or against roses? Are we for or against maths? Are we for or against telescopes? Are we for or against creation? Of course we are for creation. But when it comes to the question of human development of creation, we are for obedient response and against disobedient response. We are always for technology when it is responsible and life-giving, sensitive to God's ways. We are always against technology when it is unfolded in obedience to idolatrous perspectives.[3]

The secular mind is often striving to convince us that part of God's world is divine and part of it is worthless. This approach can only blind us. This false dilemma forces us into a cage of choices that is filled with folly. In this cage, we do not even begin to understand that technology can be redeemed. Tool-making, one of those many human activities, can be restored to stewardly service of the Lord. It is possible, if we have the eyes of faith, to develop technologies that will greatly eliminate toil and drudgery from our lives, open up rich possibilities without the concomitant curses of pollution, dehumanisation and meaningless lives. But we must always be sensitive to God's norms; we must seek the Lordship of Christ in technology.

The writer of our article is clearly aware of these kinds of problems. Some people in our culture (and sadly many children) seem to have a zombie-like existence. Their days are dominated by an endless preoccupation with video games, the speed and efficiency of their cars and a fanatical devotion to meaningless statistics. Many children hanker after expensive gadgets then, amused for only half an hour, turn restlessly to the latest horror movie. Bored and dissatisfied, they take it out on some unsuspecting telephone box.

Our writer certainly understands the lack of meaning in much modern life, but he does not open us up to wisdom. He merely blames and insults technology. She is the problem and those who praise her live in folly.

But technology is not to blame. She does not bring those curses. Our western societies are plagued with meaninglessness, fragmentation and dehumanisation because the hearts of 'modern people' have worshipped science and technology *as gods*. They have served the created and not the Creator who made the possibility of science and technology in the first place. That idolatry is the cause of a great deal of the suffering in our world.

Christian teachers can help children understand such issues, exposing false dilemmas that need to be questioned. If we don't expose them and open up a biblical response, we will encourage children to reject Christianity, since so often it seems to say very little to our highly complex world. But the gospel speaks to every possible situation, to any given problem. Our Creator, Jesus Christ, is constantly wrestling with his human image-bearers; he is always calling us to respond trustingly to his covenantal ways.

The secular mind, as expressed in this article, often presents us with two or three competing humanistic approaches that urge us to understand reality in a certain way. A powerful and prophetic Christian perspective is almost never presented. The cumulative impact of this robs children and teachers of any sense that Christianity can 'renew our minds' and open us up to fresh perspectives. Not only this but Christians are often so drenched by powerfully articulated secular positions that they begin to buy into such false dilemmas.

There are some amusing, but tragic, illustrations of such false dilemmas from medieval times. One debate centred on the delicate question, did Adam and Eve go to the toilet before the fall? Some theologians believed that Adam and Eve did not need to go to the toilet at all. Such bodily functions became necessary only after the fall. Others rejected this position and urged Christendom to believe that Adam and Eve did in fact go to the toilet before the fall but there was, of course, no smell!

Did Christ ever laugh? Some would say never; some would say occasionally, some would say reluctantly.

Did Christ experience pain and suffering on the cross? Some would say no; some would say a bit; some would say yes, but qualify this with many exemption clauses.

These issues were debated by the sharpest minds. They even consumed people's lives. In actual fact, people were being presented with a Greek pagan framework (Neo-Platonism) which encourages us to pit reason against faith, body against soul, heaven against earth, reason against laughter, church against world. This kind of framework will always drive us to ask the most ludicrous questions. Listen to Paul: 'See to it that no-one takes you captive through hollow and deceptive philosophy, which depends on human tradition and the basic principles of this world rather than on Christ' (Col 2:8).

We escape such dilemmas when we cease to concoct theories which pit one part of God's good creation against another part. If rationality is good then imagination and laughter is bad. If technology and science are so important then poetry, imagination and stewardship aren't really important. And so on.

These fruitless approaches blind us to the really important questions: how can we serve God in our thinking, tool-making, imagining, feeling, theorising and playing? How can we bring all things 'captive to Christ'? All of life should be a sacrifice of praise to our God who made the heavens and the earth; every good activity, be it painting, administration or football, should praise the name of the Lord.

As Christian parents and teachers we must begin to understand the many false dilemmas that besiege our minds and those of our children. The god of this world, Satan, is constantly seeking to mould us so that we no longer reveal Christ to the world. He often does this by cunning use of 'false dilemmas'. And textbooks are full of them!

I now want to turn to a 'ghost story'. In chapter two I argued that a spiritually exhausted humanism will always call into being a fascination with magic and the occult. Bored and disillusioned children crave excitement and purpose. Ghost stories and macabre tales of the unexpected have never been so popular. Let's have a look at a story that might well be used in an English lesson.

> Remember Samson? Met him the other night in the Cross Keys and told him where we were going to paint. He stared at me horrified, not quite the reaction I expected, so I asked him what was so peculiar and he says that place is haunted. 'Haunted by what?' I wanted to know.
>
> 'This monk,' he told me, and what is more Samson has seen it with his own eyes. He never goes round that way now but a while back he was driving towards the triangle and he felt the hair on the back of his neck go prickly and he was chilled to the bone. Couldn't understand it so he slowed down. He saw a figure up ahead, standing on the green, thought it was a woman in a long dress at first then he saw it was a monk with a cowl over his head. As Samson went by he turned to look at this fellow – he nearly crashed the car when he saw the monk had no face! He paused. 'Still want to paint out there?'
>
> I shuddered. 'I never saw anybody. I'll think about it.'
>
> It is hard to understand why we did go in the end. Separately we had been distinctly warned off and now Samson's tale reinforced this taboo. Then I thought about that lovely scenery. I am, in the cold light of reason, of the obstinate opinion that ghosts do not exist.[4]

Here we have a snippet of a ghost story. And a good ghost story it is. Exciting, well written and imaginative. But, as Christians, we need to be discerning. In the stories of ghosts or the occult that our children read, are they enabled to understand what is really going on?

Ghost stories and other macabre tales can be interpreted in at least three different ways. First, there are people who would argue that 'in the cold light of reason' ghosts simply do not exist. This position is a typically humanist response and prejudiced by commitment to that particular worldview. It urges us to take such stories with a pinch of salt.

Secondly there are people who would say that ghosts do exist and that the occult is fascinating. We can all explore that world together. If you feel like playing with an ouija board to contact the dead, then go ahead. You might even end up speaking to Elvis Presley! This position encourages the exploration of things unseen and unmentioned in traditional science textbooks.

Thirdly there are people who would say that the Bible urges us to be very careful about such matters. In contrast to our first two positions this position argues that there is indeed an unseen realm (a hidden part of creation) and that to interact with this unseen realm is to risk interaction with malevolent and destructive powers. In short a dabbler in the occult will unwittingly encounter demonic powers that seek to damage and destroy human experimenters.

Now it seems to me that a ghost story will tend to encourage belief in one of these interpretations at the expense of competing perspectives. Perhaps it will suggest that such stories are complete fabrication and invention. In that case a typically humanist perspective will be conveyed. Perhaps a ghost story will suggest that ghosts are very real and it is possible and even virtuous to contact these departed souls, chat with them, learn from them and even cheer them up. In that case a typically pagan perspective will be conveyed. It is also possible to convey a position that oscillates between humanism and paganism; a person might be highly sceptical and yet fascinated, unbelieving but willing to experiment.

It is also possible to write 'ghost stories' which open up a Christian interpretation; it is possible to delight and warn at the same time. One only has to think of Saul and the medium of Endor (1 Sam 28:3–19) to realise that such stories can be redeemed. The biblical narrative in 1 Samuel makes it clear that consulting mediums and wizards was to break the covenant and so anger God. Such practices are neither encouraged by the biblical account, neither are they understood as harmless unenlightened superstition.

It seems to me that most of the 'so-called' ghost stories I have read encourage either a sceptical or pagan interpretation of the unseen part of creation. On both positions occultic practices are understood as harmless. For humanism, a seance is harmless because there is nothing to be contacted. For paganism a seance might well promise a deepened understanding of the mystery of the universe. Both these positions do not impart wisdom to young people.

Why then do so many children seem so fascinated by ghouls, demons, ghosts and vampires? On one level it seems to me that young people crave excitement and flights of fancy that neither humanism nor Christianity (as they experience it) provide. A one-dimensional 'Industrial Darwinism' conveys a disenchanted and bleak universe. Christianity is often understood as narrow and lacking in imagination and flair. Accordingly paganism and its accoutrements can become highly seductive. Paganism and its magic and mystique will always thrive when humanism ceases to convince and Christianity has lost its distinctively prophetic and radical bite.

What should a Christian response to this be? First, we need to be humble. If 95% of the stories and plays that our children read do not open them up to a Christian worldview and its excitement then we have only ourselves to blame. Secular and pagan interpretations of life and reality are embodied in the literature our children read because secular and pagan writers and artists are working out their worldviews in every aspect of life. Christians need to integrate their faith with art and literature. Sadly, very few do. There are of course notable exceptions. One only has to think of C.S. Lewis' tales of Narnia. Here we have some delightfully imaginative fantasy stories that deftly and indirectly open children up to a Christian perspective.

Christians have a calling to create fantasy literature that is inspired and shaped by a Christian worldview. This kind of literature would affirm the goodness of imagination, make-believe, intrigue, humour, flair and mystery but within the framework of a life-affirming biblical worldview. This response would be the perfect antidote to distorted occultish literature.

As we become aware of these wider issues, we can respond

in much more immediate ways. We can explain to children and young people that there is a great deal of evidence that occultic practices can be highly destructive. Several years ago a non-Christian teacher friend of mine told me that some boys had been playing with an ouija board and one of them 'slipped off his chair and broke his leg'. My friend was not particularly open to Christianity at that time, but he knew that something destructive was going on. From that moment on his attitude towards such practices was totally different. Another friend of mine knew a girl at his school who committed suicide because she believed that the ouija board was telling her to kill herself. Such stories abound and can convince many non-Christians that it is better to stay away from such activities.

Notes

1. Andrew Carter, *English Workshop Volume 3* (Hong Kong: Hodder and Stoughton, 1980), pp 2–3.
2. Quoted in Sue O'Connell, *Focus on Proficiency* (London: Collins ELT, 1984), p 182.
3. Steven Monsma has edited an excellent book which explores how technology can be understood and practised in a Christian way. (See bibliography.)
4. Doreen Evelyn, *Our Neighbourly Ghosts* (Bradford-on-Avon: Ex Libris Press), pp 67–68.

CHAPTER FIVE

MATHEMATICS

In our western culture mathematics is often seen as completely unconnected to a person's worldview. In this view maths has nothing to do with 'religion'. This means of course that there can be no such thing as a Christian perspective on maths.

But in actual fact it is possible to teach maths in very different ways. If you examine 'traditional' maths textbooks you will often find pages and pages of algebra. It is difficult to understand how all that algebra relates to our everyday world. You simply work through your quadratic equations and that's it. But is this the one and only way to teach mathematics?

In order to understand what I mean when I say that maths can be taught in very different ways we need to look very briefly at the philosophy of mathematics. I will show that different philosophers understand maths in very different ways and that these differences have profound implications for the classroom.

When we say that $5 + 7 = 12$, what are we saying? Some philosophers have believed that numbers and numerical relations have absolutely nothing to do with this world. In this view the numerals and other symbols of maths stand for rather bizarre entities that live in an eternal realm. To put it very crudely, these pure numbers live in a heavenly realm where there is no time.

In actual fact this position maintained that these heavenly numbers were more real and more important than anything we can see with our eyes. It follows from this that mathematics is the study of divine entities and further that such study will reveal the deepest mysteries of the universe. Some of these thinkers (the Pythagoreans) believed that numbers were divine and should be worshipped.

This philosophy of mathematics is rooted in a pagan Greek worldview. Maths, as a subject, has nothing to do with this world, but somehow reveals to us a great deal of the furniture of heaven. This approach to geometry and arithmetic does not major on the practical relevance of maths. Doing maths is akin to contemplating the divine essence and such an exalted labour has no time for the earthly part of creation. This view of maths is often called the platonic position.

Other philosophers have believed that mathematics is all about the fundamental way that human minds construct the universe. Our powerful intellects structure and organise a chaotic universe in all kinds of ways. Man's mind is the source of all order, hence mathematics becomes the study of the human mind. The emphasis here is on man as creator; man is able to construct all kinds of mathematical puzzles, theories and conundrums. Here again maths has very little to say about the world we live in. Autonomous man invents maths as if from thin air. This view of maths has developed a very power-ful tradition and might be referred to as the Kantian position.

There are also philosophers who believe that maths is simply a tool by which man can cope with his environment. This perspective understands people as essentially biological beings struggling to survive in a certain environment. Mathematics tells us nothing about heaven or even the human mind; it is simply a tool that humans develop so as to master and control their environment. This view of maths is often associated with the famous American philosopher John Dewey.

Here we have three entirely different perspectives in

mathematics. (There are many other positions we do not have time to investigate.) $5 + 7 = 12$ can mean very different things to different people. But what has this to do with the practical teaching of mathematics?

I want to show that a person's underlying philosophy can profoundly influence the teaching of mathematics. I will attempt to do this by contrasting three very different ways of teaching maths. Our first approach has been developed by a group of Canadian Christians and I will call it the 'stewardship' approach. Sadly few people have ever heard of this exciting perspective. Our second approach is often called the 'traditional' approach and will be familiar to almost everyone. The third approach I will call the 'relevant' approach and some of you will be familiar with this. Let us start with a self-consciously Christian approach. An account of this perspective will deepen our understanding of the dominant secular approaches to mathematics.

The Number and Shape of Things: An Integrated Math Curriculum for the Elementary School is a fascinating Christian contribution to a distinctively Christian view of mathematics.[1] This perspective is seeking to rethink and redirect both mathematics and the teaching of mathematics at the primary school level. (Incidentally, it is interesting that teaching at the primary school level tends to be much more integrated and 'wholistic' than teaching at the secondary school level. Perhaps the lack of examination pressure allows for a more integrated approach.) At a philosophical level this perspective seeks to reject the many pagan and secular interpretations of mathematics that vie for our attention. Its basic approach, as I understand it, is as follows.

Mathematics investigates neither a divine realm of numbers, nor the human mind. Nor is it simply a helpful tool that man uses to master and control his environment. Mathematics investigates two of the many rich aspects that God's ordered world displays. The creation is multi-faceted; it is the theatre of God's glory. We can distinguish numerical, spatial, kinematic, physical, biological, sensitive, logical, historical, lingual, social, economic, aesthetic, legal, ethical and faith aspects (at the very least) in God's world. Because God has ordered and structured the creation in such a wise way, it is possible to investigate mathematical order.

Mathematics attempts to investigate the numerical and spatial aspects. It is different from, say, biology which investigates the biological aspect of creation. But maths is always about God's creation; it helps us to understand God's world.

Having established, very crudely and briefly, what mathematics is all about, we can begin to explore a much richer way of teaching it. We could begin with a project – for example, caring for animals. How do we as stewards of creation obey God in the way that we care for our animals? (Children love this as they can talk about their pets.) We need to measure precisely how much food and water is needed. To care about God's world forces us to count, to weigh, to measure, to add and to subtract. Quite simply, our hamster will die if we get our maths wrong! Good, obedient stewards need to develop basic mathematical insights.

We could turn to a different project, such as river pollution. This would demand a vast amount of mathematical activity. But it will become obvious to a child that mathematics does not tell us the whole story. Yes we can measure, count, add and weigh, but pollution, as a phenomenon, displays a host of aspects that are not mathematical. We need to sensitise children to the social, economic, aesthetic, legal and ethical dimensions of pollution. This would fascinate them as they explore God's creation as young stewards, ever mindful that his world is rich, whole and cohering.

With this approach we begin with concrete situations and develop mathematical concepts as they arise. Mathematics is then understood as a meaningful and stewardly task that we perform before God. It is not an isolated activity that seems to have nothing to do with the rest of the curriculum, but rather deepens a child's understanding of pets and his or her environment.

It needs to be stressed that this particular approach to maths does not always insist that you begin with a project! As soon as a mathematical concept arises out of a whole context, it is possible to develop theory in more abstract fashion. But theory is always presented as intimately connected to the wholeness and richness of everyday life. Theory is unfolded as servant to God, neighbour, animals and the environment; it serves and preserves the world.

Let's turn now to the 'traditional' approach. You may recall your own experience of maths. Did your maths homework look like this?[2]

Solve for x

1.	$4x = 36$	2.	$7x = 84$
3.	$12x = 156$	4.	$2x = -20$
5.	$3x = -36$	6.	$7x = -42$
7.	$-x = 10$	8.	$-2x = 18$
9.	$-4x = 36$	10.	$2x = 0$
11.	$-4x = -16$	12.	$-8x = -168$
13.	$-13x = -169$			

And so the book goes on and on. Pages and pages of algebra, equations and exercises. Cosines, concyclic points, segments, trigonometrical functions, logarithms, tangents, spheres. To be fair there is some small attempt to relate maths to reality, but by and large maths seems a world apart from everyday life.

A young person might ask why he should bother to master this impressive array of mathematical concepts. What does it have to do with his life? He might receive the answer: mathematics is a training for his mind.

But a little reflection will persuade us that our young friend is asking an intelligent question. You do not improve a person's reasoning ability by giving them a quadratic equation;

you get them to analyse arguments. Mathematics and logic are different.

This traditional approach to mathematics tends to isolate mathematical concepts from the rest of reality, thus maths becomes a kind of puzzle or game. When we ask why we are doing it we become embarrassed and confused. It does not sound very deep or impressive to say that we play these conceptual games to distract us, to amuse ourselves, to titilate our fancy. 'To improve Master Dobson's mind' sounds so much more grand and heroic.

At root this approach to mathematics is deeply coloured by a philosophical perspective that believes that mathematical activity has little to do with the world we inhabit. Perhaps mathematics can speak to us of heaven and the gods, or maybe it is the grand invention (*ex nihilo*) of man's mind. Such perspectives betray an understanding of mathematics that refuses to understand it as simply one of the many tasks that we can perform before God as humble and obedient stewards of his world.

But this is not the end of the story. Mathematics textbooks have changed a great deal even in the last five years. The emphasis now is not upon concepts, algebra and the lofty training of the mind. Mathematics textbooks are now concerned to be 'relevant', 'down-to-earth' and 'practical'. This philosophy is well expressed in the following passage:

> Over the last few years there has been much discussion about making the teaching of mathematics relevant to people's lives and work. This book attempts to do this.
>
> In part A you will find a series of practical applications of basic mathematics. Each chapter contains an introduction to the topic, a series of practical questions about the topic, a student project and some suggestions as to how other subjects can be related to the topic. Several of the projects require the student to carry out his or her own investigation, either directly, or by using information supplied by you.[3]

Without doubt the relevance of mathematics to everyday

life is stressed throughout the entire book. To some extent mathematics is shown to relate to science, social studies, career development, information technology, etc. Here is an example:

Chapter 17

The World Around Us – Representing Information

Quite often in newspapers, on the radio or on TV you are presented with statistics, such as '3½ million unemployed people', '4 out of 5 cannot tell margarine from butter', 'the Liberals got 30% of the vote'. Often these numbers mean little because you do not know the full story. Some people are frightened by numbers and cannot deal with them. In this chapter you will be looking at ways of turning numbers into diagrams by looking at comparisons between life in the UK and in other countries.[4]

This way of teaching maths is certainly very different from the traditional perspective; relevance and practicality are stressed. But it is also very different from the stewardship perspective we have briefly discussed. The stewardship perspective stresses that mathematics is to be done as an obedient response to God. The activity of mathematics helps us to love God and our neighbour, and to understand and care for the rest of creation. This 'relevant' and 'practical' approach has no such underlying thrust. On page 157 we find the following:

A Final Comment

Most people can get by in life using very little mathematics. To do this, however, you do have to trust the experts like the kitchen designer, the travel agent or the supermarket cashier. You also have to make a lot of guesses such as how much paint to buy for the ceiling – this can lead to expensive mistakes. By using some mathematics as you have in this and previous chapters you can be more efficient, more accurate and tackle more difficult problems. Think about it.[5]

Such comments reveal that maths, in this view, is only relevant and practical in as much as it can help us to cope, survive and get a job. On page 78 we are told:

> As travel and tourism become more important to the economy of the country, more jobs are becoming available in travel agents, information centres, etc. The work in this chapter could be useful if you are thinking of applying for this sort of job.[6]

Does this mean that if a young person does not intend to apply for this kind of job they don't need to study this chapter? Is education only preparation for life in industry? Such questions begin to reveal the bankruptcy of this pragmatic humanism. I would like to suggest that this approach to mathematics is strongly coloured by a worldview that believes that maths is simply a tool by which autonomous man can cope with his environment. A position that is just as secular as the traditional approach.[7]

In this chapter we have contrasted three very different approaches to mathematics. The traditional view of maths tended to stress the training of a person's mind; man is a dignified and noble creature and the study of mathematics enables him to contemplate eternal truths. This position betrays an optimistic humanism. More recent maths teaching tends to stress mathematics as a tool by which man can cope with his environment. This position is much closer to what I have called pessimistic humanism. It would seem yet again that a much more pragmatic and 'survivalist' humanism is gradually beginning to dominate our culture and our schools. Both these humanistic approaches contrast strongly with our stewardship alternative that presents mathematics within the context of obedient service to God.

Notes

1. *The Number and Shape of Things: An Integrated Math Curriculum for the Elementary School* Calvin Jongsma

and Trudy Baker (Toronto: Curriculum Development Centre, 1973).

2. A J Raven, *Mechanical Mathematics Book 1*, (London: Heinemann Educational Books, 1972), p 81.

3. L Farrow & S Llewellyn, *Mathematics: Using the Basic Skills* (Cheltenham: Stanley Thornes Ltd, 1987) from the Introduction.

4. *Ibid* p 134.

5. *Ibid* p 157.

6. *Ibid* p 78.

7. I am indebted to Roy Clouser for many of the ideas in this section on maths.

CHAPTER SIX

TECHNOLOGY

We have already touched upon technology and its place in our modern culture. The recently proposed National Curriculum places design and technology in the 'foundation subject' category. Education Secretary Kenneth Baker has recently said:

> Design and technology are vital areas of the curriculum. They are of great significance for the economic well-being of this country. I believe it is essential that we press ahead quickly in establishing them within the National Curriculum.[1]

We do not have space in this short book to investigate all the many facets of design and technology. I have selected *Collins Guide to Modern Technology* by Robin Kerrod as a general introduction to the subject. This is how the book starts:

Introduction

About two million years ago our primitive ape-like ancestors in Africa began to make tools by chipping flakes from pieces of flint. In so doing they took a gigantic leap forwards along the path to civilization. They had begun to invent things, a trait that set them apart from the other animals. They had begun to alter their environment for their own benefit. And ever since human beings have been improving their lives by making practical use of their discoveries and inventions – in other words, by technology.[2]

To most people this would seem a purely 'factual' account of human development. But is it? When we begin to scrutinise the content of this passage we discover that it is written from the perspective of an optimistic humanist.

This writer believes, with commitment and faith, that our 'primitive ape-like ancestors' began to shape and mould civilisation by making tools. This ability to make tools distinguishes man from the rest of the beasts. Such ability to invent and alter their environment allowed the human race to take a gigantic leap towards civilisation. He shares the simple faith of the Enlightenment philosophers. Autonomous Man's great ability to control and transform his environment will bring him the promised land.

The writer's unquestioning trust in this life-perspective becomes clearer as he continues. He points out that technology has a dark face as well, citing 'the terrible hydrogen bomb', but his faith in the human conquest and mastery of the earth is unshakable.

> We now have what appears to be the ultimate weapon – the terrible hydrogen bomb. But perhaps even this is not all bad. The prospects are good that, with advancing technology, we shall be able to control the energy-producing process behind the bomb. And that could mean abundant power for the whole world for the foreseeable future.[3]

In the writer's view, advancing technology, further research and more control of the environment will solve the overwhelming problems of mankind.

In a seemingly innocuous passage from a book on technology we are presented with a highly humanistic perspective on life and the universe. For a man or a woman who is committed to a biblical worldview, this passage is quite simply false. It strongly suggests that man is not a dependent servant of a great God, subject to his laws and ways, but an autonomous controller of his environment. It suggests to us and our children that we will live securely in the land by trusting in the power of our technical mastery.

This stands in stark contrast to the Christian worldview. Here, humans will only live securely in this life – and the life to come – if they trust and obey their Creator and Redeemer, Jesus Christ. This means that all of life, including technology, must honour the Lord and his purposes for this world. For this world does not belong to autonomous and technically brilliant animals; it belongs to Christ.

Why is it that if a Christian perspective is articulated with any commitment and vigour, many teachers and parents object on the grounds that it is indoctrination? Yet nobody becomes even slightly concerned if a particular brand of atheism is promoted. Somehow an atheistic faith in 'progress' has become so much an accepted part of our modern world that adherence to this particular atheistic faith is simply 'normal', 'objective' or 'commonsensical'. In this view the dominant religion or worldview (faith in scientific and technical progress) is deemed factual and uncontroversial. Competing life-perspectives (Christianity, Buddhism, Hinduism, Judaism or Islam) are biased, irrational and highly controversial. The unwitting public are actually being indoctrinated into one particular life-perspective. And when that worldview claims to be 'unbiased', 'neutral' and 'objective', it will have a tremendous advantage over competing life-perspectives.

Notes

1. K Baker, *News* (London: Department of Education and Science, April 29 1988), p 1.
2. Robin Kerrod, *Collins Guide to Modern Technology* (London: Collins, 1983), p 4.
3. *Ibid*.

CHAPTER SEVEN

GEOGRAPHY

Acid rain is a topical issue, one which could well be addressed in a geography lesson. Typical treatments of acid rain are well worth exploring. I have chosen the book *Acid Rain* by John McCormick.

Introduction

An acid blight is spreading across the Earth. Rain, snow, fog and mist, polluted by the smoke and fumes given off by factories and cars, are being turned acid. This 'acid rain' is gradually wearing down our environment, affecting countries in almost every continent. It attacks and damages our buildings and monuments. Forests are dead or dying. Soils are turning acid, wildlife dying, crops are being lost. Lakes are emptying as their populations perish in rising acid levels.... In this book we will look at what acid rain is, why acid pollution is a problem, and what can be done to control it.

Polluted skies
Acid pollution is caused by the smoke and gases given off by things like factories, cars and lorries, that run on fossil fuels like coal and oil.... These pollutants pour into the atmosphere along with smoke.[1]

In this passage we are informed about the effects of acid rain, and then told that such environmental problems are caused by 'the smoke and gases given off by things ... that run on fossil fuels like coal and oil.' Fair enough. You can't argue with that.

Can you? Just as our biology textbook reveals an impoverished and reductionistic understanding of sexuality, so this book presents an approach to acid rain that is equally impoverished. This way of understanding acid rain does not reflect true wisdom. Listen to the prophet Hosea:

> Hear the word of the Lord, you Israelites,
> because the Lord has a charge to bring
> against you who live in the land:
> 'There is no faithfulness, no love,
> no acknowledgment of God in the land.
> There is only cursing, lying and murder,
> stealing and adultery;
> they break all bounds,
> and bloodshed follows bloodshed.
> Because of this the land mourns,
> and all who live in it waste away;
> the beasts of the field and the birds of the air
> and the fish of the sea are dying.'
>
> Hosea 4:1–3

It is clear from the prophets and the law that unfaithfulness to God and his laws of justice, stewardship, love and righteousness will bring a terrible curse upon the face of the earth. When humans reject God's covenant, preferring autonomy to obedient stewardship, then the curses of sin and idolatry will rise up and strangle us. The land will mourn, humans will waste away, and the animals will die. Isaiah puts it like this:

> The earth dries up and withers,
> the world languishes and withers,
> the exalted of the earth languish.
> The earth is defiled by its people;
> they have disobeyed the laws,
> violated the statutes
> and broken the everlasting covenant.

> Therefore a curse consumes the earth;
> its people must bear their guilt.
>
> Isaiah 24:4–6

Just as the Baal religion believed that prosperity and peace could only come by trusting in Baal, so modern man is convinced that the good life can only come if he conquers the earth with his technical power and rational insight. Accordingly he becomes autonomous and unleashes his aggressive power upon the earth. But the fruit of his lawless mastery of his environment is the death of his environment and his fellow creatures.

Man's rebellion against God actually frustrates his deepest desire to live securely in the land. Acid rain is not an inevitable consequence of industrial progress. It is a sign that the human race must repent of its disobedient autonomy. It is a sign that our aggressive and lawless mastery of the earth is doomed to fail. Above all, it is a sign that man cannot live by bread alone but by every word that comes from the mouth of God. Psalm 24 comes to mind:

> The earth is the Lord's, and
> everything in it,
> the world, and all who live in it;
> for he founded it upon the seas
> and established it upon the waters.
> Who may ascend the hill of the Lord?
> Who may stand in his holy place?
> He who has clean hands and a pure heart,
> who does not lift up his soul to an idol
> or swear by what is false.
>
> Psalm 24:1–4

What, then, is the solution to acid rain? Is it simply to pour money into research? Is it to pay more scientists to invent better technology to clean the rivers and forests? Of course, there are physical and chemical aspects to this phenomenon, and a responsible and life-giving technology and science should be developed to tackle them. But we must recognise that not all problems can be solved by greater efficiency and control of nature. The ultimate solution to such serious problems is to turn away from a humanistic worldview that stresses autonomy and mastery and to rediscover the biblical themes of stewardship and servanthood. It is to rediscover the meaning of our life in serving – God, spouse, neighbour and environment (Genesis 2:15).

The heart of the Gospel, the death and resurrection of Jesus Christ, offers us a way of turning from idolatry and living in this world in ways that please God. Then our hearts will delight in the preservation of the land, each other and obedience to God's ways. In this approach, science and technology would be unfolded as a stewardly response to God, not as the means of salvation.

It is possible to develop an understanding of pollution and acid rain that does not divorce the physical and chemical dimensions of the problem from the many other aspects. Children need to know that there are legal, ethical, social, economic, aesthetic and spiritual dimensions to the problem. For example, both animals and humans experience distress when their habitat suffers; we need to discuss the responsibilities of business companies, banks and other institutions to God, their neighbour and their environment. We need to instill in children a deep sense of the interconnectedness of life and the many inter-relationships of the world around them.

Governments have a calling to legislate just laws which encourage responsibility and discourage greed and poor stewardship. What might this mean in terms of concrete policy proposals? We must also explore the responsibilities we have towards future generations. Then there is the important issue of international justice. If one country creates acid rain it may well affect neighbouring countries. To what extent is our response to such issues dominated by nationalism? These important questions can be raised in any context.

The aesthetic and social damage caused by such pollution merits consideration. Dead fish in murky rivers and dead seals in polluted seas are not a pretty picture. Equally unsavoury are houses, located near 'toxic' waste dumps, infested with flies. By raising such questions we will guide our children and ourselves towards the paths of wisdom that God longs for us to follow. We will also help our children to understand that all individuals and institutions have responsibilities as stewards and servants of the earth.[2]

We can help children and young people to develop a richer understanding of pollution in very different environments, both hostile to and supportive of Christianity. For instance, we might adopt the 'Socratic method' where we ask appropriate questions to elicit an understanding of acid rain or the 'greenhouse effect' that goes way beyond the confines of a secular textbook. In doing so we will open their eyes to the richness and coherence of God's world, and underline the inadequacy of a reductionist approach where explanations are limited to physical and chemical causation and little else.

Notes

1. John McCormick, *Acid Rain* (London: Franklin Watts/ Aladdin Books, 1985), pp 4–7.
2. Alan Storkey is currently working on an approach to economics in which he develops this theme of the servanthood of institutions in a very interesting way. Individuals, families, banks, educational institutions and governments etc all have callings as stewards. (See bibliography, in particular Storkey's book *Transforming Economics*.)

CHAPTER EIGHT

HISTORY

Let's now turn to a history textbook which deals with the Spanish conquest of Peru in the 1530s. I have chosen this passage because it deals with European and non-European cultures as they interact with each other. History should not just be concerned with English history but the history of many different civilisations and their impact upon each other. (I will deal with some 'English history' towards the end of this chapter.) This passage is also of interest in that it conveys Christianity in a particular light.

> The days of the Inca empire were about to end. News of the arrival of strange, bearded men in the country came just as the emperor Atahuallpa emerged as the victor over his half-brother Huascar in a civil war which had weakened the empire. Atahuallpa did not take the threat seriously enough until it was too late. The vast Inca empire fell to a small army of Spanish soldiers and adventurers who had come to seek their fortunes in gold....
>
> Atahuallpa camped outside Cajamarca with an army of 30,000 men. At first all seemed to go well. The emperor offered the strange newcomers chicha beer and agreed to eat with them the next day. That night Pizarro cunningly hid his men around the square in Cajamarca so that it appeared to be deserted. When Atahuallpa arrived he was met by a Spanish priest reading from a prayer book. The book was handed to Atahuallpa who examined it and then threw it away. He did not understand what it was, nor how holy it was to the Spaniards. This was the opportunity they

had been waiting for. As the book touched the ground, Pizarro's hidden army, shouting their battle cry 'Santiago', attacked and Atahuallpa was taken prisoner.

The captive emperor

For eight months the Spaniards held Atahuallpa captive, but they allowed him to rule and to have his wives, servants and courtiers about him. Several of the Spaniards were fascinated by this glimpse of Inca life. Others were horrified by it. At last Atahuallpa, realizing how much the Spaniards wanted gold, offered to pay a fabulous ransom to buy his freedom. He would fill his prison cell with gold as high as his hand could reach. He kept his word, to the delight and amazement of the Spaniards, but it did not save him.

As long as Atahuallpa was alive, he was a threat to the Spaniards, who feared that the Incas would attack and free him. They accused him of several crimes and condemned him to be burned to death. To save himself from this fate, so that his body could be properly preserved like those of his ancestors, Atahuallpa agreed to become a Christian. On 29th August 1533 he was baptized and then strangled....

Under Spanish rule

The conquest was a disaster for the Incas, destroying their way of life, their religion and their pride. Spanish priests began at once to convert the new subjects of the King of Spain to the Roman Catholic faith. Those who resisted were harshly punished, often with torture and death. Some people were baptized but many of these, not understanding the meaning of what they had done, still paid homage to their gods. They were also severely punished by the Spanish rulers who had little sympathy for their customs.... The Conquistadors were often brutal masters. They forced people to work until they died, especially in the mines.[1]

In many respects this is a valuable account of the Spanish conquest of the Incas. It seems sensitive to the brutal way in which the Spanish Conquistadors effectively destroyed the

Inca civilisation. But does this treatment of the Incas and their Spanish conquerors give us wisdom about what really happened? Yet again it seems that we are subjected to a minimalistic and impoverished account.

Consider, for example, the way in which Christianity is treated in this text. There seem to be three occasions where Christianity is brought into the story. First we are told that the Spanish contrived to trap Atahuallpa by giving him a prayer book; they felt confident that this king of the Incas would commit some unforgivable faux pas and so justify their wicked schemes. Secondly we are informed that Atahuallpa agreed to become a Christian so as to avoid the ignominy of a burnt corpse. Such a 'conversion' permitted Atahuallpa to die a more dignified death: he was merely strangled. Thirdly we are told that 'Spanish priests began at once to convert the new subjects of the King of Spain to the Roman Catholic faith. Those who resisted were harshly punished, often with torture and death.'

What is being conveyed to children by this passage? How will a typical child respond? 'If that's Christianity,' thinks he or she, 'then I'm not interested. Such a religion disgusts me.' Many children can be put off for life by such an account.

Just as the Baal religion had merged with true biblical religion, destroying the true way by transforming the genius and beauty of God's ways into a squalid and trivialised cult, so Christianity for Pizarro and his friends had become a grotesque and ugly affair.

The truth of the matter is that Pizarro and his Conquistadors knew nothing of Christianity. As Scripture puts it, they had exchanged the glory of God for something disgraceful. They claimed to bring the gospel to a dark continent, but they actually brought something even more disturbing than Baal worship. In their prayers they whispered praises to Jesus and the blessed Virgin Mary, but their lives proclaimed allegiance to a different god. And that god was Mammon. Those Spanish Conquistadors were men driven by greed and lust. Men who would do literally anything for money or power. They lived out a vision of life that they called Christian, but they actually served the father of all lies.

We know from Scripture that God calls us to live a life of righteousness, love and justice. He calls us to show unbelievers his greatness and majesty, to reveal Jesus Christ to the nations. But what do we discover in the life of Pizarro and his soldiers? Something extraordinarily sordid and corrupt. A Christianity that found some profound meaning in a prayer book; a Christianity that burned the heretic; a Christianity that tortured others.

A responsible and truthful account of this episode in history will help children to understand the simple fact that these Conquistadors disgraced the name of Jesus as they cheated and lied to the Inca people. We need to open the eyes of our children to the word of God:

> But godliness with contentment is great gain. For we brought nothing into the world, and we can take nothing out of it. But if we have food and clothing, we will be content with that. People who want to get rich fall into temptation and a trap and into many foolish and harmful desires that plunge men into ruin and destruction. For the love of money is a root of all kinds of evil. Some people, eager for money, have wandered from the faith and pierced themselves with many griefs.... Command those who are rich in this present world not to be arrogant nor to put their hope in wealth, which is so uncertain, but to put their hope in God, who richly provides us with everything for our enjoyment. Command them to do good, to be rich in good deeds, and to be generous and willing to share.
>
> 1 Timothy 6:6–10, 17–18

Further, such an account of the Conquistadors will help children to understand that any mixture of Christianity with pagan or secular perspectives, such as the worship of money, power or reason, robs the gospel of its power and uniqueness. Children will reject the gospel if they are presented with a trivial and contemptible distortion. The passage we have examined makes no attempt to alert a child to any of these problems. There is no hint that Christianity might speak powerfully to other areas of life other than just holy books and religious ceremonies. Christianity becomes by definition a rather odd and irrelevant perspective.

This brings me to my second point. There are indeed many different ways in which history can be written. Competing 'meaning-frameworks' guide and prejudice the historian. All historians, whether they call themselves religious or not, investigate and explore the past in terms of their fundamental life-perspective. They select those facts they deem significant, thus leaving out a great many others. Hindu, Marxist, Progress and other kinds of 'meaning-frameworks' guide and penetrate the account an historian will give of any particular historical epoch. For example, some historians write history in terms of man continually improving himself. The history of the world is the story of the advancement of man. Many years ago man was very primitive; then he advanced a little and became more adept. When he discovered science and technology he progressed in leaps and bounds. At the end of the twentieth century man is becoming astonishingly brilliant, and perfection seems near. He looks at the past with a smirk and a mocking smile. All shall be revealed as progress is surely ushered in by the forces of reason.

Such a perspective interprets life and the past in a particular way. It is reluctant to convey fully the horror of modern war and its devastation. But this view of history has had a deep impact upon us all. Somehow we have been persuaded that history is the glorious march of human reason and technical mastery. Such philosophical prejudices are often lurking behind the most innocent document.

Another perspective on history tends to present it as a succession of one fact after another. History is simply a meaningless affair of event after event. This perspective often claims to be 'presenting the facts' and thereby to shun interpretation. But by understanding history as a meaningless ebb and flow, it is prejudiced at a fundmental level against the perspectives we have called Progress, Marxist and Christian.

A scholar's life-perspective will always deeply colour her understanding of the historical process. It is for this reason that we should not be surprised to discover that some historians display a deep contempt for Christianity. If someone believes in the power of 'progress' to bring wholeness and peace, then that person will despise the belief that only Christ and obedience to him can bring the promised land.

In the light of such considerations it becomes not only possible but essential to develop a Christian approach to history. I shall very briefly sketch the contours of such an approach and then explain how I would teach the story of those Conquistadors in the light of a Christian philosophy of history.

First it is crucial that history is understood in terms of God's call to the human race to unfold and develop his world as faithful and loving friends. We are creatures whom he has commanded to 'multiply and subdue the earth'; to open up the surprises and mysteries of his world and develop culture and civilisation. Our goal is not an uncultivated garden but a splendid city full of redeemed art, comedy, music, dance, scholarship, sport and everything else that enriches human life. Do not imagine for a moment that the Heavenly City will cure us of insomnia. It will be 'creation regained'; the fulfilment of the promise of creation. All the surprises and possibilities of creation will delight us there as we enjoy everlasting friendship with God the Father, God the Son and God the Holy Spirit. Not only the Lord but the angels, animals, plants and rocks will love us. Alienation, despair and boredom will vanish for the heavens and the earth will be full of the glory of the Lord.

But we know that human beings have not unfolded these surprises that beckon us to the glory of God. We know, if we listen to the groanings of creation, that human rebellion and satanic intrigue encourage the human race to pervert those marvellous gifts and surprises. We know just how distorted creation can become as idolatry grips the hearts of those called to image the King. Mankind has lost his way. He needs to rediscover the radical and cosmic redemption God has given us in his Son. He needs to rediscover that God loves his world.

It is within this context that history takes shape. History studies this human response to God's call to the human race. In history we seek wisdom as to how humans develop the earth. We focus upon the development and unfolding of, say, European culture. Not only do we examine this historical process but we try to discern the difference between obedient and disobedient responses to the Lord. We attempt to discover and understand both the kingdom of darkness and the kingdom of light in the very warp and woof of the historical process. A great deal more needs to be said but there is no space to further these sketchy suggestions.

Let us return now to those Conquistadors. How might we present this episode in terms of our Christian perspective? First, I would try to explain to the children that there are different approaches to history. I would contrast the perspective of progress with the biblical one. You would begin by saying that ten thousand years ago life was terrible and everyone was miserable. Gradually this changed as man got the measure of the world. Now everyone is happy. Most children will dispute this. A good discussion can ensue in which the advantages of modern life can be contrasted with the disadvantages. You would then move on to discuss the Roman Catholic Spanish culture that produced the likes of Pizarro. You would need to stress that many sincere priests undertook some fine work among Indians where the true gospel was preached and lived out. The film *The Mission* could be discussed. In particular you could talk about the different approaches to mission that the film explores. It is not difficult to help children to understand that Christianity can be relevant and exciting – and that it can also be distorted.

This film will also stimulate discussion about Spain and

Portugal *vis à vis* South America. The teacher can introduce the biblical theme of response. All people at all times are responding either obediently or disobediently to the Lord's 'cultural mandate'. The Spanish people were no different. The Incas also developed culture. We are all of us, whether we like it or not, tied up with a particular culture. We can then begin to analyse the distortions and evils of both cultures. The Incas worshipped their pagan gods, sometimes sacrificing people to their sun-god. The Spanish church and government also burnt 'heretics' at the stake. Both cultures were tarnished by idolatry. Christianity is then understood as a perspective that challenges *both* the Spanish and Inca cultures.

From an initial interest in the Incas and their Spanish conquerors we begin to trace fascinating connections with a host of gripping issues. When children grasp that issues of culture, geography, history, philosophy and religious commitment are intimately connected, they will be encouraged to learn and read. History is no longer a blur of meaningless facts, but a significant and integrated subject.

For example, how do we understand the Industrial Revolution? Why was nineteenth-century England so different from medieval England? This is an intriguing question. In a history lesson we can explore the beliefs of thirteenth-century English knights and barons and contrast them with the beliefs of nineteenth-century factory owners. We will discover that medieval people tended to understand their ultimate future as in heaven. This belief did not encourage innovative technical and scientific exploration. Somehow a person was just passing through; earth was but a shadow of heavenly glory and there wasn't much point in becoming too at home 'down here'. In contrast to this, many nineteenth-century factory owners couldn't give a fig for such pious talk. Life and its meaning becomes much more earthbound in the light of progress and 'Enlightenment'. The future is not heaven, it is material prosperity for a limited time on earth.

History makes much more sense when we begin to understand the worldviews and commitments of different periods. A culture breathes a spirit (or a Zeitgeist, as the Germans call it) and history needs to test and discern these spirits.

To really get to grips with Roman history we need to do more than just memorise a few facts about Julius Caesar. We need to get inside the mind and heart of a gladiator or a Roman soldier or a tribune or an emperor (Caligula) who has just made his horse a consul. To accomplish this we need a grasp of the Roman worldview. Roman history makes much more sense when you begin to understand the beliefs and commitments of the Roman citizen.

To teach history in this way can be done just as easily in a comprehensive school as in a school where it is easier to be honest about one's Christian commitment. In my experience children prefer this approach far more than the dominant one which tends to neglect worldviews and the 'spirit' of a particular culture.

Note

1. Anne Millard, *The Incas* (London: Longman Group Limited, 1980), pp 38–40.

CHAPTER NINE

RELIGIOUS EDUCATION

The 1988 Education Reform Act seems to reaffirm strongly the place of religion in our schools when it comes to the part of the curriculum designated as Religious Education and School Worship. Classroom RE is not part of the National Curriculum but in county and voluntary controlled schools it must continue to be provided as part of the basic curriculum for *all* registered pupils, whatever their age, according to locally decided 'Agreed Syllabuses'. One of the new requirements under the Act is that any new Agreed Syllabus must 'reflect the fact that the religious traditions in Great Britain are in the main Christian whilst taking account of the teaching and practices of the other principal religions represented in Great Britain' (Education Reform Act 1988 Part 1. Section 8(3)). This would appear to mean that Christianity must be the central component, but that non-Christian faiths must also receive some treatment.

For a Christian, however, concern over Religious Education is not simply an issue of how much time should be spent on Christianity. Deeper issues are at stake. What precisely is Religious Education? What impact does it have upon children? Is it simply a 'Cinderella' subject as many claim?

In this chapter I would like to highlight certain key themes that dominate the way RE is taught in our schools. Let's start with a book called *Thinking for Life*. The introduction tells us this.

This book is about forming opinions. It differs from many other textbooks in use, which are concerned primarily with facts. Not that there are no facts in this book, far from it. We are going to touch on many facets of life where understanding facts is necessary. The more careful consideration of the facts the better, for the opinion drawn will be more balanced. But this book is concerned primarily with ideas. We are continually asking 'What does this mean?', 'How will this affect the quality of life?', 'What of future generations if we do this or that?'.

Exercise

Consider the subjects on your timetable for this year and in previous years. Which seem to you to be: primarily factual; primarily a matter of opinion; a bit of both – in what quantities?[1]

This passage expresses a dominant theme in our humanistic culture: there is a realm of facts and there is a realm of opinions or values. Science tells us the facts, and ethics or Religious Education tells us about the values. Almost every textbook I have examined as a supply teacher makes this distinction between certain facts and uncertain values. This belief that reality can be sliced up into two such worlds can be extremely damaging to one's Christian faith. To understand why, we need to look at some historical background.

This expression – facts and values or facts and opinions – goes back to the philosophical school of neo-Kantianism which was prominent in Europe in the late nineteenth and early twentieth centuries. Its thinkers have had a profound influence upon textbooks, particularly RE textbooks.

According to these thinkers, 'facts' were things which could be objectively and certainly known: physics, chemistry, maths and biology would reveal to us verified or certain knowledge which could not be challenged. 'Values' on the other hand were creations of the human mind and simply expressed how humans felt about the facts.

The insightful Christian thinker Albert Wolters continues the story:

It is a 'fact' that water freezes at 32°F and to think otherwise is to be mistaken. But it is only a 'value' to believe that crime should be punished, or that adultery is wrong, or that Jesus is the Christ. About such matters you can think differently, but you cannot be wrong. Facts are true no matter what, values can be said to be 'true' only in the sense that they are widely held in a given society or period of history. The religious distortion in this view is obvious to every child in the body of Christ, for it is God, not man, who is the law-giver.

Nevertheless, the influences of this neo-Kantian distinction, pushed largely through the social sciences at the universities, has been so great that today most Christians are unwilling to speak any longer of 'divine ordinances' or even of the 'moral order' as they used to in the nineteenth century. Instead they refer to their Christian 'values', thereby implicitly conceding the point that their convictions on these matters do not have objective validity or factual status. Because of this prevailing talk of 'values' and all that this implies, it has almost become impossible for a Christian, especially in an academic setting, to believe that 'thou shalt not kill' is every bit as much a fact as 'water freezes at 32°F.[2]

Such 'value-judgments' as 'rape is wrong', 'racism is evil', 'killing innocent people is acceptable', 'destroying the environment is wrong' do not convey any 'factual' knowledge in this particular humanistic perspective. Such opinions merely express your feelings. They have nothing to do with the facts. This way of understanding the world, as Wolters says, has been propagated by many universities and colleges; many a student is taught to distinguish between factual statements and value-judgments.

In the 1930s a group of philosophers, known as the 'logical positivists', developed a view of ethics which declared that all statements that intended to convey ethical judgments were simply nonsense. If a statement did not convey a factual content, it was deemed cognitively meaningless. (This philosophical perspective is now extremely unpopular and outdated.)

What impact does this perspective exercise upon the teaching of RE? Religion, in this view, is simply a matter of personal preference. It all depends on human opinion and value-judgments, so you can't be wrong. Or right. Only facts can be right or wrong, and RE isn't about facts, it's about human values. If you want to find facts you must go to the scientist.

What is the effect of this approach upon children? My experience has been that many children tend to feel rather contemptuous towards all the so-called world religions. If religion is simply a matter of personal preference and you can't be wrong or right then religion simply becomes a big joke, or something akin to choosing the colour of your car. Worthy of a few moments' consideration, but basically unimportant. In modern and secular cultures religion is often perceived as odd and embarrassing.

Behind all this we need to notice that Christianity, Buddhism, Islam and Hinduism, as worldviews, are all judged (in much modern RE) by humanism and are found wanting. These perspectives are considered to be prescientific and unenlightened. Listen to the following definition of theology in *Thinking for Life*:

> *Theology*. This word means both 'words about God' and 'taking rational trouble about God'. Some of man's finest insights and deepest aspirations are to be found in the religious texts of the world. This raises another serious question: How can we have a religious set of values today? The great world religions were formulated a long time ago: how can we achieve anything like the spirituality recorded there? How can we have a sense of adoration, or a sense of having done wrong, or how can we become people of meditation in a world which cannot in honesty go back to pre-scientific ways of thinking?[3]

In this passage 'religion', 'spirituality' and 'values' are understood in terms of the Enlightenment. Man has come of age; he has a scientific outlook and he cannot return to pre-scientific ways of thinking. This means that Christianity, Islam, Buddhism and Hinduism must be redefined so as not to offend the 'enlightened' ear. They are trivialised and watered down so that they do not offend the humanist. But by losing their genuine distinctiveness and radical call they actually become insipid and unchallenging.

Let's turn now to a typical treatment of Buddhism. Always, it seems to me, Buddhism, Christianity etc are so presented that they are not allowed to challenge the dominant perspective – humanism.

'The Buddha never found fault with other people's beliefs. He would never debate with people in order to put them down or to make himself appear clever.... In time, he believed, every person could find Enlightenment. Enlightenment would come when people at last understood what the Buddha called the Four Noble Truths.'

THE FOUR NOBLE TRUTHS

1. All is dissatisfaction or suffering
2. The cause of all dissatisfaction is desire
3. The cure of all dissatisfaction is to rid oneself of desire
4. The way to rid oneself of desire is by following the Eightfold Path[4]

In this passage we gain a very succinct and helpful summary of the Buddhist worldview. Suffering and misery in life is caused by desire and the Eightfold Path will extinguish all desire and lead a man or woman to Nirvana or heaven. We are also told that the 'Buddha never found fault with other people's beliefs'. But is this true?

In actual fact Buddhism, as a worldview, disagrees profoundly with both the Christian and humanist worldviews. In a typically humanist perspective desire is not something to be extinguished but encouraged. Autonomous man desires to control and conquer his environment and this will bring him the good life – abundant material consumption. A consumer society strives to convince all people that they desire all possible consumer-durables constantly. Such a society begs you to discover desires that you never guessed you had. For example, you need a car with cruise control. Don't you? For a committed Buddhist this western preoccupation with the stimulation of desire ruins your prospects of gaining Nirvana. Why? Precisely because Nirvana will be gained by those who learn to free themselves from the demands of desire by the appropriate moral and meditative techniques. In a Christian worldview desire can be redeemed; desire is twisted and distorted by sin and idolatry but it can be redeemed through Christ. I can desire with all my heart that God's presence will fill the earth!

Imagine the following scenario. A huge multi-national corporation and its location. Over night, seven of the leading managers become Buddhists and start to study *The Dhammapada*. They begin to take it seriously. They begin to realise that the encouragement of consumption and desire is not the best way to live in the world. They approach the shareholders of the company and urge them to initiate reform in the light of the Buddhist worldview. The shareholders believe in consumption and the need to stimulate desire. They reject this proposal and sack the converted managers.

What we need to understand here is that a humanistic worldview will only tolerate Buddhism (or any other competing vision of life) if it learns to behave itself. Humanism always 'de-fangs' any competing worldview by restricting the scope and relevance of 'so-called' religion.

The practical impact of this upon the teaching of RE is to 'interpret' Christianity, Islam, Hinduism and Buddhism as worldviews that have almost nothing to say in 95% of what we call life. Such religions speak to us about colourful festivals, 'confirmation', special diets and days of celebration. They may offer us guidance in our personal morality. But they have almost nothing to say about the direction of 'public' areas of life: industry, politics, economics, scholarship, engineering, banking, sport, insurance and architecture are all unfolded in the light of a humanistic worldview. If Christianity and the other religions will behave and conform to these public directions then humanism will smile upon 'religion' and tell her what a good girl she is being.

When we investigate treatments of Christianity and the other world religions in typical RE textbooks we tend to find that 'religion' is all about ceremonies, diets and unusual customs. This treatment, accordingly, *marginalises* these perspectives. They are only allowed to address personal or private issues. In short, religion is all about the realm of values; it is merely a matter of opinion. It does not really impinge upon the public realm of facts which is the realm of truth and falsehood.

Let's now look at some typical treatments of Christianity. I have selected a textbook called *Christianity Then and Now* by Richard Hughes:

The disciples were in a boat half-way across the sea of Galilee when night fell. Suddenly, they noticed Jesus walking on the surface of the water towards them. They were very frightened, believing that they saw a ghost. 'Take heart,' said Jesus. 'Lord, if it is you,' said Peter, 'bid me come out to you on the water.' 'Come,' said Jesus. Peter set off on the surface of the water. He succeeded until he took fright. Then he began to sink. 'O man of little faith,' said Jesus as he rescued him. 'Why did you doubt?' When they had got into the boat, the disciples went down on their knees before Jesus. 'Truly, you are the Son of God,' they said.

This amazing incident, described in St. Matthew's Gospel, shows that the writers of the New Testament meant more than one thing by faith. Faith certainly meant trust. The story shows us that anyone who trusted in Jesus could do the miraculous things that he did. But faith also meant belief in all that Jesus stood for. The disciples believed all Jesus' teachings because of the miraculous powers that he showed.

Stories such as this one had a different effect at the time when they were written, from the effect they have now. The scientific background of modern thought has meant that we are sceptical about superhuman actions of this kind. Such stories discourage belief in us almost as much as they encouraged belief in the people of the first century. The author of St. Matthew's Gospel was writing for the people of his time and knew what would appeal to them.[5]

This passage illustrates how Christianity is adapted and transformed in the light of humanism. The so-called 'scientific' worldview does not allow us to believe in such 'superstition' as Jesus walking on the water and so we must assume that the 'author of St. Matthew's Gospel was writing for the people of his time and knew what would appeal to them'.

What is going on here? At root we are being presented with the bias and prejudice of an Enlightenment worldview. Somehow something called 'science' provides us with an infallible body of certain factual knowledge. This body of certain factual knowledge does not include even the possibility of 'walking on the water' and so we must conclude that the gospel of St Matthew is full of error and invention. Accordingly, anything in the Bible which does not comport well with this so-called 'scientific' worldview must be rejected. This is, of course, a dominant theme in 'liberal theology'. This approach encourages us to believe that anything in the Bible which offends the modern ear can be dispensed with. The Bible is not allowed to challenge modern humans and their societies. It is merely a very fallible and very human record of primitive and pre-enlightened belief.

What should a Christian response be to this?

I believe that the Achilles' heel of this particular brand of humanistic faith is being best exposed by humanists themselves. A great debate is raging in the history and philosophy of science. Science does not provide us with a certain body of established dogmatic fact. That is a primitive view of science. It is a much more human and fallible activity than we had thought. Science itself is plagued with uncertainty and prejudice. It is constantly changing. Theories come and go.

There is a growing recognition among philosophers and scientists that this thing we call 'science' does not reveal to us an incorrigible body of verified fact. Science itself is shaped and moulded by beliefs and prejudices. This means of course that it is quite mistaken to claim that science 'disproves the Resurrection' or that 'modern science has conclusively proved that angels do not exist'. Such credal statements simply express faith in an old-fashioned view of science that demanded faith and obedience to a mechanistic and materialistic view of reality. There are even those who declare that 'science' has become a highly uncritical and dogmatic institution. The famous philosopher of science, Paul Feyerabend, puts it like this:

> Thus science is much closer to myth than a scientific philosophy is prepared to admit. It is one of the many forms of thought that have been developed by man, and not necessarily the best. It is conspicuous, noisy, and impudent, but it is inherently superior only for those who have already decided in favour of a certain ideology, or who have accepted it without having ever examined its advantages and its limits. And as the accepting and rejecting of ideologies should be left to the individual it follows that the separation of state and *church* must be supplemented by the separation of state and *science,* that most recent, most aggressive, and most dogmatic religious institution.[6]

Here we can appreciate the wisdom of a humanistic thinker who is deeply critical of 'science as revelation'. The prejudice and bias of the liberal theologian and the Enlightenment intellectual are beginning to be exposed.

As Christians we need to understand the 'hidden agenda' of RE textbooks. More often than not Christianity is taught in the light of a dogmatic faith in science. The expression 'the scientific perspective' seems so innocent, yet it conceals a host of dogmas, commitments and assumptions that are hostile to the Christian worldview.

The impact of such teaching upon children is devastating. They are encouraged to be highly critical of the Bible and sceptical about anything that is not 'scientific'. Children are simply told, on authority, that such and such is unscientific and therefore not to be believed. This initiates them into a way of understanding the world that gives ultimate authority to science and its supposed infallibility.

Behind all this we would do well to understand that a

humanistic faith in science, reason and human technical power is being conveyed to our children. Yet again a dogmatic faith in 'Enlightenment' belief and vision is being foisted upon an unsuspecting and trusting generation of children.

Notes

1. Tom Gardner, *Thinking for Life* (London: Edward Arnold) p 1.
2. Albert Wolters, *Ideas Have Legs* (Toronto: Institute for Christian Studies, 1987), pp 6–7.
3. Gardner, *op cit*, p 2.
4. Dilwyn Hunt, *Leaders of Religion: The Buddha* (Edinburgh: Oliver and Boyd, 1987), p 25.
5. Richard Hughes, *Christianity Then and Now* (Oxford: Oxford University Press, 1981), pp 64–65.
6. Paul Feyerabend, *Against Method* (New York: Schocken Books, 1978), p 15. I would like to add here that I do not fully agree with all that Feyerabend says. His critique of a dogmatic faith in science is powerful but I believe it is possible to develop a very positive understanding of science that arises out of a Christian worldview.

    For a very helpful account of the recent loss of faith in science and its seeming infallibility, see A F Chalmers, *What Is This Thing Called Science?* (Milton Keynes: Open University, 1986). This book develops a good critique of verificationist, falsificationist and sophisticated falsificationist accounts of science. The book is weak, however, in that it fails to develop a convincing alternative.

CHAPTER TEN

ART

Normally speaking, art in the curriculum refers to the visual arts: drawing, painting, pottery and sculpture. Apart from studying the history of art, or as sources for visual ideas, textbooks are rarely used in art lessons, so I will not refer to any in this chapter.

As we have seen, one of the significant points about contemporary education is the tremendous lack of coherence. Art teachers often feel cut off from other teachers. What on earth does art have to do with maths and biology? They may also feel undervalued and misunderstood. Some people say that art as a curriculum subject is unnecessary – 'merely a frill'. It is not 'practical' and 'productive'. Other people believe that art is the most important activity in life. To engage in art is to become semi-divine. Clearly, some people tend to depreciate the importance of art while others over-value it.

The National Curriculum does make place for art as a foundation subject, but at the same time it seems to stress science, technology, computer studies and preparation for work. How should Christians respond to this?

At the outset we need to understand that the role of art in our modern world is highly ambiguous. In terms of the fact/value distinction, which we discussed earlier, art tends to be placed in the 'value' sphere of life rather than the 'fact' one. In an art lesson, then, you do not receive 'factual' information; you paint and draw. And what does that have to do with the 'real' world?

In the philosophy of art and aesthetics, a leading question concerns the meaning of artistic activity. What is art and what does the artist do? If we follow the thinking of materialist philosophers and educationalists, who tend to construe reality in terms of mathematical, physical and chemical conglomerates, then art becomes highly problematic. If the real stuff of life concerns mastering and controlling 'nature', then art becomes merely a self-indulgent game, an amusement to distract you from the meaningless of 'matter in motion'. At the very most, it can become a willing slave of industry. Once we have mastered our environment and produced the consumer-durables, we need to persuade people to buy and consume our products. So we tap the artistic gifts of men and women to create clever commercials.

On the other hand, if we follow the thinking of those sympathetic to the 'romantic' movement, art and artistic activity are the only truly meaningful things in life. To engage in art is thus to become a superior being, unsullied by contact with commerce or science.

Herman Dooyeweerd has argued that modern secular humanism is often torn between the pole of freedom and the pole of science. Some humanists are wary of an emphasis on science and technology because it threatens to control man and rob him of his freedom and dignity. Other humanists, such as BF Skinner, so stress science and technology that man does indeed lose his freedom and dignity, for science and technology control and determine him.

In art we can observe a similar theme. There are those who construe art as servant to scientific and technical progress, while others stress the complete freedom, dignity and genius of the Great Artist. For Dooyeweerd both positions are cursed by the humanistic worldview. Man must either abandon his desire to dominate and control, or abandon his freedom and dignity. But autonomous man wants both!

In contrast to both the above views is the Christian understanding of reality. While sharing the belief in a real imaginative and aesthetic dimension expressed by the second viewpoint, Christian thinking includes a God who calls humans to shape and develop the potential of creation which includes the use of artistic gifting.

In considering the place of art in the National Curriculum, we need to ask some preliminary questions. Why is art important? And how should art and artistic activity fit into a school curriculum?

To begin with we need to recognise that we all spend time and money watching films, plays and cartoons: we all read newspapers, novels and comics. We buy furniture, rugs and vases. We live in houses and flats. We visit cities and towns. All kinds of people have designed, shaped and moulded these different things. To speak of cities, buildings, towns, films and vases is to speak of men and women who draw, scheme, imagine and paint. Drawing, painting and designing is a necessary part of all these responses to the Lord's cultural mandate. The house, flat or office where you are presently reading this book was designed by one person or group of persons. They have contributed to your life in an important way. Let's imagine for a moment that drawing, scheming and painting have been eliminated from the cosmos. Where would you be now? Outside in the pouring rain without even the hope of an umbrella!

What I am trying to convey is the simple truth that there is an aesthetic aspect to everything we encounter. I remember many years ago a three month period of my life when I became a bus conductor. I would spend many an hour in the canteen, sipping coffee, listening to the stories and enjoying the occasional poached egg. That canteen had been designed by someone, and that someone was singularly lacking in wisdom. Aesthetically it was a nightmare. The ugly paint inspired graffiti, the floor was so designed that it encouraged abuse;

slot-machines, plastic tables, plastic chairs and plastic flowers attacked my tired senses. Wit, sensitivity, subtlety and flair were not welcome in that canteen. I was not reminded of heaven on earth.

The person or persons who designed that canteen were shaping and moulding God's creation in ways that flagrantly dishonoured his intentions. A healthy sense of style, colour, variety, appropriateness and coherence were completely lacking. As stewards those designers had failed; they had not invested their talents in the kingdom of God.

Perhaps they had been influenced by the philosophy of an architect such as Le Corbusier who believed that buildings were 'machines for living in'. People thus became little mechanical units conditioned by their surroundings. Put such folk in neat, sterile and streamlined boxes and in due course they will grow up to be neat, predictable, streamlined people. But how wrong he was!

So many schools and factories are lacking in all the ingredients of good art and design. I have walked into many a school to be greeted by greyness, drabness and anonymity. To be fair I have also taught in primary and junior schools where colour, style and imaginative projects enrich the atmosphere.

Art, as a subject, should heighten children's awareness of the hidden aesthetic delights of God's world.

> The wings of the ostrich flap joyfully,
> but they cannot compare with the pinions
> and feathers of the stork.
> She lays her eggs on the ground
> and lets them warm in the sand,
> unmindful that a foot may crush them,
> that some wild animal may trample them.
> She treats her young harshly, as if they were not hers;
> she cares not that her labour was in vain,
> for God did not endow her with wisdom
> or give her a share of good sense.

> Yet when she spreads her feathers to run,
> she laughs at horse and rider.

Job 39:13–18

Could you paint or draw this foolish, laughing ostrich? Could you capture the ostrich running or burying her head in the sand? As young stewards of God's creation, children should be invited to explore and develop the possibilities of materials and develop their sense of design. These skills, learned in art lessons, can then be practised throughout life. After all, we are made in the image of a Creator God.

Artistic activity is to be distinguished from, say, mathematical activity (adding, subtracting, multiplying, etc) because it should display subtlety, imagination and nuance as its dominant features. This is not to suggest that maths should be conducted in a sombre and unimaginative way. Or that art has nothing to do with a creative use of maths in designing patterns and shapes. Far from it. But when a child paints, draws or shapes clay, artistic stewardship calls for a different focus than mathematical stewardship.

I hope by now that it is quite clear that what I have tentatively called artistic stewardship is just as valuable as mathematical stewardship and vice versa. Art is a calling from the Lord and it concerns a particular way in which we shape and mould the creation. In this context it becomes absurd to construe art as a servant of productivity, commerce or technology. At the same time art should not be understood as the exclusive endeavour of sublime Bohemians. It is simply a calling and as such should neither be depreciated nor overvalued. A positive Christian view of art will make children sensitive to the rich aesthetic surprises of God's world and this in turn will help them to love God, each other and themselves. They will experience something of God's shalom. They will appreciate that God made the rainbow because he liked it.

As Christians we need to understand that children and young people long for *aesthetic satisfaction*. Children love to play with paints and clay, or dress up and use their imagination. This is quite normal and healthy.

But so often children experience school as unimaginative and aesthetically stultifying. Young people often complain that school is boring; the world seems to lack mystery and adventure. The goal and purpose of life is ambiguous. Perhaps getting a job, the possibility of marriage, or a holiday in the sun. But of anything deeper little seems to be said.

A sterile humanism will always call into being a fascination with the occult. Games like Dungeons and Dragons become popular in the context of a meaningless materialism. This kind of game, full of incantations and occultic dreaming, re-enchants reality for children. As the thirteen-year-old son of one Christian mother recently said, when questioned about his interest in Dungeons and Dragons, 'I'm bored at school. It gives me something to look forward to.'

Children who are starved of redeemed imagination will escape their disenchanted lives by constant day-dreaming – of the capricious Madonna or the pouting Maradona. Of the lives of stars who seem to enjoy endless leisure, perpetual foreign holidays and unlimited sex. Many children have no time to read and study; their lives are too emotionally draining, their minds too full of romantic escape.

It is very revealing to examine the kinds of pictures that children tend to draw and paint. My experience has been that they go for vampires, demons, ghosts and graveyards. On one level they believe the humanistic worldview as transmitted by their textbooks but in a curious way they also believe in astrology, magic and tales of the unexpected. Somehow humanism and paganism need each other. The public allegiance to science, technology and economic growth (materialism) often hides a very private allegiance to superstition, astrology and contacting the dead. It is almost as if the very sterility and meaninglessness of contemporary idolatry forces modern man to oscillate between the worship of himself (humanism) and the worship of the pre-enlightenment gods (paganism). And in art lessons this ambivalence can be clearly seen.

The antidote to this must recognise the goodness of imagination, subtlety and creativity in all of life as a humble and loving response to God. It must also recognise that some people are specifically called to be cartoonists, film-makers or painters. Such gifted people have a powerful impact upon our world. The artists who create cartoons, advertisements and 'video-nasties' shape you and your children.

We must honour these callings in much the same way as we honour pastors and evangelists. If we fail, then our children will be condemned to spiritual death because they will only have access to films, plays and cartoons that convey secular and pagan visions of life.

We also need to appreciate that the aesthetic aspect of God's world can be integrated into all the other subjects. We can teach French, for example, in a much more imaginative and artistic way than it is often done. I recently saw a group of children in a comprehensive school performing a play in French that they had written. And much to my surprise it was a great success. The play was funny, entertaining and full of mischievous sound effects. There were lots of visual jokes and puns that the children had invented themselves. Speaking French became enjoyable because the aesthetic aspect was integrated into its teaching. It was exhilarating to see children who normally claim to hate French loving it. It contrasted strikingly with the approach to language learning that concentrates almost exclusively on grammar – amo, amas, amat.[1]

Note

1. This chapter on art was the fruit of a communal struggle. Janice Russell and Ian Cotton helped considerably in the development of many of these ideas. We are also indebted to Calvin Seerveld and his marvellous book *Rainbows for the Fallen World* (Toronto: Toronto Tuppence Press, 1980).

Conclusion

This section has covered some of the areas now prescribed under the National Curriculum. We have examined a wide range of different textbooks. We have discovered that these textbooks are deeply prejudiced by commitment to a humanistic worldview. Implicitly and explicitly school textbooks promote and foster a way of seeing the world that is hostile to the biblical vision of life. We could say that these books tend to anaesthetise children to such biblical themes as atonement, prayer, providence, creation, fall, redemption, idolatry, justice, stewardship, shalom, righteousness, faith, love, wholeness and servanthood. Such themes mean little to the dominant worldview of our culture which rejects the living God and his call to the human race.

What, then, is the Christian response to this discovery? I have tried to indicate briefly a positive Christian alternative, but it has only been in passing. Parents will need to consider carefully the view of the world which their children are receiving through their predominantly secular education. It is only in understanding this that they can begin to understand *why* their children are acting, talking and feeling in a certain way. It is only as we unmask the hidden assumptions behind our children's curricula studies that parents can begin to build up an alternative worldview and present a biblical perspective of what the world, wisdom and knowledge, people and happiness are all about.

In the next section we will explore what various Christians are doing to rethink and redirect education.

Part Three

A Christian Response

Now that we have some understanding of the biblical worldview, idolatry, humanism and the dominant perspective enshrined in typical textbooks, we can begin to explore some of the many things that Christians are doing to rethink and redirect education in the light of a biblical view of reality.

In the following section teachers and educators will speak for themselves. What do they struggle with? How do they teach? For some the content of the curriculum is explored; for others the way in which we teach is examined. Some of our contributors are teaching, or have taught, in primary schools; some in comprehensive schools; some in sixth-form colleges, and some in independent Christian schools.

This section is in no way intended to prescribe what Christian teachers 'ought' to be doing. It merely shares the experience of various teachers. They show that it is possible to teach within a variety of school situations applying one's own understanding of a Christian perspective to one's professional responsibilities. Their experience will, hopefully, be an inspiration to Christian parents as they seek to discuss their children's studies with them, and open them up in a new way and with a new understanding. The experiences of these teachers may well stimulate other teachers to consider their own subject and the way they could be teaching it from a Christian perspective within the particular school situation in which God has placed them.

One does not have to agree with everything that is said by these teachers and educationalists. There is no uniformity in a Christian approach to the curriculum, and this part of the book, reflecting diversity, is intended to encourage us all to think through these issues for ourselves, drawing upon the wisdom God provides.

CHAPTER ELEVEN

SCIENCE

To teach science in a way that is illumined by the biblical worldview requires a great deal of reflection. Our modern secular culture has convinced most of us that 'science' has nothing to do with 'religion'. It is completely neutral, objective and unshaped by religious prejudice. In this book I have tried to show that this is completely mistaken. Science, be it chemistry, physics or biology, is always practised in the light of a person's worldview.

Arthur, who is now living in Bolton, has spent many years teaching science in different schools. He has thought very deeply about questions of curriculum and science. Of particular interest is his concern to develop an understanding of science that is opposed to 'reductionism' and stresses the many important interrelationships that God's world displays. The central impulse of scientific understanding should lead to responsible stewardship and not lawless mastery. Arthur relates three particular areas that he considers important in teaching science.

First he explains the need for science teaching to demonstrate the interaction between different realms of the world. Secondly he helps us to discover the assumptions made by certain scientific statements. Thirdly he emphasises the importance of spelling out the specific 'role' played by any one entity studied in science, and of demonstrating that in its particular context it is ideally suited to play its role and contribute to the balance of the whole.

Interaction

In every science subject we should start with the largest realm, or context, of meaning. In biology we should start with the world of life as a whole (ecology), not with cells or biochemistry. In chemistry and physics we should start with the non-living world around us (from galaxies to rocks), not with atoms and particles. Only then can we give every thing its proper meaning – or discover the extent of our ignorance! In considering the various entities within a science subject, we would do well to discuss these questions:

(1) What is the role and purpose of the particular entity in its proper context?

(2) What is its significance for me – what are the implications for my role? In what ways do I hinder or uphold its role? (The full import of 'serve and keep' (Gen 2:15) is 'carefully and responsibly practise God's word for all of life through obedient service.')

In relation to the Earth, any science course must keep the seven interacting realms of the world (figure 2) firmly in the foreground. They show that the inhabitable and hospitable condition of the world is the result of the carefully designed and dynamic interaction between these realms. Following on from this, we must not undermine the unity of meaning by wrenching things from their context, nor disintegrate that meaning by treating things as nothing but a sum of separate parts, eg organisms as a sum of organs or genes, air or seawater as a sum of chemicals.

Let us focus on the latter for a moment in order to drive this point home. From the standpoint of the physical sciences, the

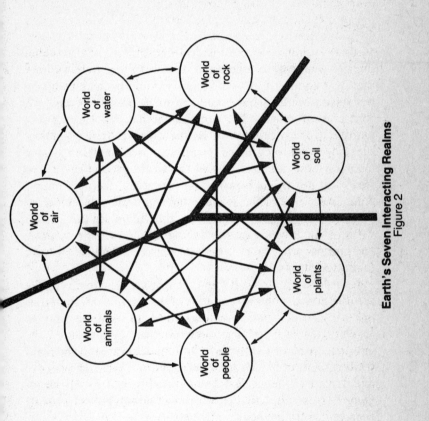

Earth's Seven Interacting Realms
Figure 2

Non-living Realms

Living Realms

World of water

World of rock

World of air

World of soil

World of animals

World of plants

World of people

most important thing to be said about air and seawater is that they are quite impossible mixtures! (But how many textbooks say so?) For example, the oxygen and nitrogen in air are very reactive elements. Under Earth's warm, moist, sun-irradiated conditions, their overwhelming tendency is to combine with other elements to attain the most stable forms – oxides and nitrates. If chemistry alone applied, the Earth would eventually settle down to an equilibrium state with a hot, high-pressure, reducing, carbon-dioxide atmosphere (like its sister planet Venus whose conditions can now be presented as more than just another fact). The oceans would be acid, reducing and salt-saturated. There would be no life possible of any sort. The present remarkably constant 'unnatural' state is due entirely to living organisms. By their high activity organisms speed up the slow cycles of the physical world and in so doing maintain both themselves and the world around them in a steady state (homeostasis) far removed from chemical equilibrium. All of this is quite amazing when we remember that the living world is just a very thin 'scum' on the Earth's surface! This is where we should base our knowledge about air and oceans rather than on a list of component chemicals with their properties and uses.

And we cannot leave it there; people are also involved. We are now converting vast amounts of the Earth's raw materials into forms suited to our own activities. In so doing we have accelerated parts of the slow physical cycles and have interacted violently with the fast cycles of the animal and plant worlds. God, in his wisdom, created these cycles in order to maintain an optimum environment for his creatures by means of processes and activities which are noiseless, low-energy, economic, self-balancing and self-cleansing.

But in our rebellion, we have proceeded in such disregard of the Creator's laws that we have created a system that is so far from optimum that it is unsustainable. Our world-system is now being shaped by activities that are noisy, high-energy, brutal and wasteful. We are squandering the non-renewable resources of God's world at a phenomenal rate and producing vast amounts of pollution. Given this situation, we are irresponsible if we do not explore our responsibilities as accountable stewards of God's world with our children. To do this we cannot avoid crossing subject boundaries and tackling social, economic, political, ethical and religious issues. An adequate teaching of any subject should lead relentlessly to an integration of them all.

Assumptions

In deciding which is the most advanced country in the world, do we automatically weigh up the claims of such nations as the USA, Germany and Japan? If so, what criteria are we using and why? Are criteria of economic or scientific and technical attainment adequate? American agriculture, for example, is judged to be highly efficient because it produces such huge surpluses. But if we use 'energy requirement' as a criterion, American agriculture, being high-energy, may well be the most inefficient on Earth! When we compare energy input (fuel, fertilisers, etc) to energy output (food calories) we find an agricultural system that is only sustainable as long as America can command far more than its just share of world resources. Now I am certainly not commending either criterion. The point I am making is simply this: if the way we present so 'straightforward' a topic as fertilisers carries assumptions, then we can be sure that all other topics do as well.

This leads us on into a major illustration of the way in which worldviews affect our understanding and presentation of science, namely, the way in which we use scientific/medical/technical interventions to evade and cover up activities that go against God's norms in the social, political, economic and ethical dimensions of life.

For example, we tacitly regard the human body as a complex biochemical machine and so respond to illness with a drug-centred health service, plus surgical interventions. But illness almost invariably has many other dimensions beyond the biochemical. We would do well to remember that social and environmental change, such as improvements in nutrition, hygiene and sanitation, have had a much greater impact on health and life expectancy than medical intervention. But it comes down to the individual too:

– We much prefer the impersonal tablet or injection to a probing of our living habits and lifestyle and the possibility of being confronted with unhealthy behaviour.

– We would rather promote condoms than face the thorny question of sexual morality whose unpalatable answer would immediately halt the spread of AIDS.

– We would rather abort unborn babies because of 'social disability' than tackle the necessary social reforms.

– We would rather spend millions on medication for hypertension and stress (and in responding to the concomitant increased incidence of heart disease, cancer and diabetes) than challenge and change the overcompetitive business world.

– We would rather respond to Third World problems with high finance, high technology and birth control programmes (pills and devices again). In that way we don't tread on any sensitive toes and we retain our 'influence' with the countries concerned (ie with the ruling élites). But Third World problems are often primarily matters of all-pervasive national and international injustice grounded in non-Christian worldviews – both ours and theirs.

Sadly we must confess that many Christian missions share in the guilt. This discussion could be extended indefinitely and doubtless many of my comments are open to debate. But the point I am making is a general one. Issues such as the ones we have discussed above all surface in modern science courses. What assumptions do we make in the way we, or the textbooks, present them? Are we preparing our children to develop and practise a true and prophetic critique of their world? Or do we leave them without wisdom?

Role-centered teaching

We must avoid teaching in linear series, especially supposed evolutionary series which falsely suggest that some elements are 'lower', 'more primitive' and 'less efficient' than others. Research continually and consistently affirms that, in relation to its own proper context and role, each element is an optimum solution to the problems of life and existence. Implementing this in teaching requires a particular emphasis.

– The different kinds of animals and plants should be considered in relation to their ecological and community roles rather than primarily in terms of classification and recognition.

– Animal and plant cells would become far more than a list of similarities and differences if we considered the way cells function and hence the need for these two different types of cell if plants and animals are to fulfil their complementary roles.

– Carbohydrates, fats and proteins should be presented in relation to their differing roles in respiration, food transport, food storage, water production, buoyancy, etc.

– The chemical elements should be considered first and foremost in relation to their roles in the different realms of the world, eg hydrogen as the key element for stars, oxygen for planets, silicon for rocks (its absence or near absence in many school syllabi is quite revealing), aluminium for soils, nitrogen as atmospheric dilutent (the proportions of oxygen and nitrogen are quite critical: at less than 14% oxygen no fire could be lit, but at 25% even wet vegetation burns), sodium, potassium and chlorine ions for maintaining the concentration of the Earth's fluids (oceans, seas, body fluids) as they do not react or precipitate with any other common substances, and so on.

The different 'forms' of energy can be considered in relation to the different requirements of the different kinds of created thing. For example, the key importance of chemical (food) energy in the functioning of living things, but of nuclear energy in stars. The distinction between amount and kind of energy is also important. If the sun's surface was only 550°C and the Earth was much nearer, the climate would be very similar to what it is, but the energy of the predominantly long-wave radiation would be quite insufficient to sever chemical bonds and life would be impossible.

The same approach – concentrating on role and function – should be applied to cold-blooded and warm-blooded animals, herbivores and carnivores, plant life cycles (annual, biennial, perennial), fungi and bacteria as decomposers, types of seed and pollen dispersal, types of vertebrate heart structure, coniferous and deciduous woodland, sexual and asexual reproduction, fish with and without gas bladders, the mechanical structure of root and stems, water-dwelling and air-dwelling (in relation to the different properties of air and water), compound and camera eyes, external and internal skeleton, etc.

CHAPTER TWELVE

BIOLOGY

In the previous chapter we saw how the biblical worldview can be integrated with science teaching. With this fresh in our minds, we move on to hear from Trevor. Trevor, who lives in Nottingham, is sensitive to the 'hidden messages' of science textbooks. Fully aware of the influence of secular perspectives upon science teaching, he responded in a very interesting and unusual way, as he explains below.

A biological message

My first teaching post was in a large comprehensive school, in a biology department with six other teachers. The teaching was well organised with the junior forms taught from a series of home-made booklets prepared by different members of the team. The quality of these was very good and they were most effective in conveying key biological ideas through a number of specific examples.

The first-year booklets centred on the theme of the variety of life and in the second term the work was based on a systematic study of the vertebrates. The pupils started this study by looking first at fish and then moved on progressively through amphibians, reptiles, birds and mammals. In each case the key characteristics of the group were studied alongside a more detailed examination of one or two specific examples. The whole thrust of the study was evolutionary and as the pupils worked through the booklets the underlying message was 'look how good fish are at turning into amphibia' and so forth. The syllabus was in effect a celebration of evolutionary change, although there was no explicit teaching of the theory. It was a classic example of teaching through hidden messages whereby a controversial theory formed the unquestioned framework of the pupils' studies.

As a young teacher I was not really aware of this framework. The quality of the work developed by the department obscured, for the probationary teacher whose main concern was to get through the next day, the worldview or perspective that this teaching transmitted. It was something I never questioned until I started taking a first-form class for RE, and I discovered that there was an inbuilt resistance to learning in that subject which I had not experienced in the safe havens of the laboratory. The basic problem seemed to be that the pupils found the key concept of religion, God, to be one that simply made no sense to them. As maturing first years they had outgrown God, Santa Claus and the other childish concepts which they left behind them on leaving primary school.

Further investigation revealed that the problem was being compounded by the substantial programme of integrated studies that was part of the first-year curriculum. One major component of this was a study of the early history of the world and in particular the evolution of our species. One of their textbooks had a picture of the stages in this evolutionary story, with an ape on the left-hand side of the page and a fully-fledged *Homo sapiens* on the right-hand side. My own eight-year-old, on seeing a similar picture recently, automatically concluded that these stages were comparable to a snake changing its skin, or the metamorphosis of a tadpole into a frog. The time scales involved and the complexity of the underlying theories are beyond the comprehension of either an eight- or eleven-year-old unless they are carefully and deliberately taught. This, however, was not the case in my school and the power of the hidden message was such that the pupils automatically assumed that the process was inevitable, unguided and within the time spans of their own experience.

Little surprise, then, that one first-year pupil commented to me in an RE lesson that God couldn't have created the world because they had learnt how it had happened in integrated studies. Few secondary teachers stand back from their own subject to look at the messages that are being conveyed to the pupils through their experience of the whole curriculum. Teachers and their pupils have totally different experiences of the school curriculum in a way that is not so for those in primary schools. Teachers suffer constant exposure to one or two subjects; pupils are bombarded by a variety of studies. Inevitably the pupils will find an integrated message to hold these in some form of unity. Because of the fragmented way in which we design the curriculum these powerful messages are invariably the unspoken and unplanned ones. For these first years one of those messages was that life is a chance phenomenon, something that has developed through a process of unguided evolution. None of my colleagues would ever have said this openly to their pupils, indeed a number of them were Christians and would have been horrified at the thought, but the way we put our curriculum together meant that our pupils imbibed (learnt is not the accurate way to describe the process since it bypassed their critical faculties) this particular message. And it implicitly undermined their confidence in God.

I was fortunate to have a Christian colleague in the biology department. Together we raised this issue of implicit messages at a departmental meeting, and particularly the responsibility of the first-year booklets in this matter. Understandably our suggestion that somehow the biology syllabus was affecting the pupils' religious development was greeted with incredulity. Teachers trained in the separate disciplines model find it very hard to understand the notion that all knowledge is part of a worldview. However, because there were two of us and we persisted, we were eventually given the task of modifying the booklets in a way that was biologically acceptable but didn't carry an implicitly anti-religious message. Obviously we couldn't turn the booklets into a philosophical consideration of the nature of knowledge, but the solution in our secular school turned out to be relatively straightforward. We simply looked for another biological principle that could be taught through a study of the variety of life, but which did not carry an implicitly anti-God message. We used the principle of adaption so that the booklets now conveyed the notion 'look how good the fish are at being fish' and so on. This perfectly acceptable biological message is compatible with, reinforces even, the Christian belief in the Creator God. The biology we taught was still secular in the sense that we didn't talk about the Creator in a way that we would do in a Christian curriculum, but it was a secular study with a very different message.

CHAPTER THIRTEEN

HISTORY

Many teachers are unaware that they *could* develop a Christian perspective to their subject. For most teachers it is simply natural that they should continue in their school to teach the view of that subject received through their predominantly secular training. Ann was teaching history in a secondary school in Kent when a pupil challenged her to think through the way she was teaching her subject. She explains.

'You're a Christian, aren't you?' The question came from a lively fourth-year girl. 'Why doesn't it show in your history teaching?' She went on to explain how my Christian commitment showed up against that of my colleague who was teaching RE.

I went home and thought hard. My Christian faith was no secret in the school. I took assemblies, led the Christian Union and was very involved with pastoral care. But the truth remained that these activities were peripheral to the main purpose of my place in the school – teaching history.

Two years before this encounter I had listened to a talk on a Christian approach to academic subjects, and was unimpressed, deeming the speaker to have an unreal view of what was possible in the classroom. Now I found myself confessing to

God that although I acknowledged him as the Lord of history in the pulpit, the classroom was a different matter. My view of history was not particularly God-honouring – and might even turn out to be God-denying.

For the first time I stopped to think about what view of history I was teaching, perhaps more implicitly than explicitly. I decided that for the less able it probably came across as the Henry Ford view – one damn thing after another. The more able were probably left with the view that Man is progressing as time proceeds. Neither perspective accords with the biblical view that creation, the fall and redemption have implications for all people, events and time, and therefore human history and the school curriculum subject of history.

So what was I to do? First I approached my Christian head-teacher with my dilemma. She could not help me to work out my own teaching programme but she offered to support me as I felt my way.

With the first years I decided to look at what history is, using their own ideas and pointing out the significance of the birth of Christ for our whole dating system. We had some amazing discussions as to why this is. By doing a lot of work on historical method, looking at evidence and bias, the pupils were opened up to the idea that discoveries can be interpreted in different ways and that we have to try to understand how people of other times and cultures might see things as well as those living in the Western world today.

We looked at periods of history such as the Middle Ages, the Reformation and the seventeenth century and tried to understand the significance of the church and Christian belief in those times. There was some excellent debate on why things are so different today.

For the sixth form, the course included a look at the history of ideas, the impact of the Enlightenment, and how today different schools of thought, such as the Marxist, bring their own assumptions to the fore in an open and honest attempt to construe history according to their own worldview. Within this context we then attempted interpretations according to our own presuppositions which enabled me to share my Christian perspective.

This is by no means the definitive Christian approach to teaching history, but it enabled me to be more true to my faith in the classroom.

The school's first graduate read history in a department that was solidly International Socialist. She testified that the way she had been taught enabled her to understand and challenge such a heavy bias. She became a Christian many years later and concluded that the 'open' way she had been taught history was one link in the chain.

CHAPTER FOURTEEN

MODERN LANGUAGES

Let's turn now to modern languages. Dave comes from Bristol and he teaches French and German in a very large comprehensive school. Dave is full of imaginative ideas about teaching and very perceptive about the GCSE (General Certificate of Secondary Education). I interviewed him recently.

Mark: Tell me what's going on in modern languages teaching?

Dave: A while ago modern languages were not the 'in' thing. Latin or classical Greek were the important languages to learn. The emphasis here was the training of the mind and grammar was excessively important. More recently people began to say that modern languages were important but the emphasis was still on grammar. French and German became more popular but they were taught in a similar way to Latin. In this approach you focus upon the grammar. It's highly abstract and unrelated to the real world. 'O' level French sums it up. 'La plume de ma tante' and 'conjugate "prendre" for me, Watson,' etc.

In the late sixties and early seventies many teachers became dissatisfied with this and began to explore approaches that stressed fluency and conversational ability; grammar became less important. At the same time there was even a danger in the mid-seventies that modern languages were going to disappear completely! Many people came to believe that the British didn't need to learn modern languages because the English language was so dominant.

Since then there has been a renewed interest in modern languages and at the same time a continued move away from the traditional approach. The name of the game is now 'communication not accuracy', whereas accurate grammar was the essence of the old approach. In spite of this new shift in language learning the requirements of 'O'level forced people to teach in the old way. You simply had to teach people in the traditional way if they were to pass the exam. The 'O' level exam in French or Spanish was geared towards correct grammar; 'accuracy not communication' was the name of the game.

This has all changed now with GCSE. The emphasis has completely switched from accuracy to communication.

Mark: So what you are saying, Dave, is that the GCSE philosophy prefers communication rather than accuracy and the old 'O' level philosophy prefers accuracy of grammar rather than the ability to communicate?

Dave: That's right. With GCSE there is far less emphasis upon grammar; you do deal with grammar but in a much more passive way. You don't teach a point of grammar and then 'exploit' it with a host of exercises. You learn about something and then at the end of a particular phase you might ask the pupils if they have noticed something. They might say that all the words about girls have got 'la' before them and all the words about boys have got 'le' in front of them. And you say, 'Fantastic, make a note of that!' Grammar is caught not taught. It's not a matter of teaching language via grammar, it's learning grammar via the language.

Now we might think to ourselves that this method of teaching is better – but there's always a sting in the tail with these things. There is very much the sense that the future economic prosperity of Britain is to some extent related to having linguists who can exploit the opening of the tunnel and the dropping of the trade barriers in 1992 in Europe. There is also a growing awareness that other countries will not continue to tolerate British reluctance to speak their languages. Helmut Kohl said last year that if the English were not prepared to come and promote their stuff in German then the Germans would buy from other countries who were prepared to speak their language! There is a growing realisation that Britain needs linguists. But sadly this renewed interest in modern languages seems to be fuelled much more by concern for economic growth and industrial efficiency than anything else.

There is also a swing in schools towards integrating the whole curriculum with information technology. Languages are suddenly becoming computer-orientated, with use of word-processors, etc. While it is exciting and challenging to use modern methods for language learning, we have to be very discerning: they should enrich our teaching; we should not serve them as 'hi-tech' commodities. But it seems to me that the government simply wants people who are competent to use these machines and it has no real interest beyond that. I'm concerned that the interests of big business could ultimately impoverish and distort modern languages teaching.

Mark: Perhaps we could pause here and sum up what's been said so far. The old view tended to understand the process of language learning as a training of the mind. But there has been a move away from this old-fashioned rationalism; the new emphasis is pragmatism! In this approach we are not particularly interested in, say, memorising precise grammatical structures of Latin. Our approach is now much more relevant and pragmatic: learning French and German won't so much train your mind as train you for industry. Do you think that this distils something of the philosophy behind GCSE?

Dave: Well, I think that broadly speaking you're right, but the content of GCSE, the topics, the exam, etc, are geared much more towards survival in a foreign country in really practical and useful ways. As yet it isn't particularly business-orientated. The National Curriculum has made languages a foundation subject in secondary schools. Most schools used to allow children to drop a language at 14, but the National Curriculum requires all children to continue with French, German or whatever until 16. This prospect is quite daunting for language teachers. Until now they haven't had to teach the unmotivated pupils any further than 14. But it's also a very exciting and challenging prospect. We have to make our teaching interesting for them. But again, the government's motivation is not that it will be good for the children; but rather we need linguists in order to survive in the industrial juggernaut.

The government says that we need 'diversification'; this means that we need an equal proportion of schools that are teaching French, German, Italian, Spanish, Russian and Japanese as a first language. It's not very difficult to see that the underlying motivation is to build business people to run the economy.

Mark: How does TVEI (Technical and Vocational Education Initiative) relate to all this?

Dave: In languages, it seems that TVEI is gearing children up to cope with language needed in business. So language is used in conjunction with computing.

Mark: Do you think it is fair to say that this is a highly instrumentalist approach to language learning? The older kind of humanism – rationalism – was instrumentalist in its own way. It wasn't really interested in the richness of the language in the context of God's world; the logical/grammatical structure was all that was crucial. Now we are concerned about the possibility of future jobs in Paris or Tokyo – and the chance of getting one if you make the effort to learn the language. As Christans we need to be discerning. No one would want to say that giving people skills that will help them get a job is a waste of time, but when you reduce education to being a servant of business and industry, you have a lot of problems. Education becomes nothing more than just training someone for a job that will boost the economy.

Dave: Yes, a school can simply become a sausage-machine. In the kind of school that I am teaching in, which is a fairly working-class area, if you say to the children that in five years time they will probably be using the language abroad, they just laugh you out of the room. They'll say – 'Our ma's never been out of Bristol, Sir! I's never going to leave Bristol!' You just can't gear your teaching towards that kind of mentality or philosophy – you can't get away with it with these kids.

Mark: How, then, do you relate your Christianity to language teaching?

Dave: Well, first I reject the perspectives that tend to reduce language learning to a 'training of the mind' or a 'training for industry'.

Secondly, I try to make my lessons enjoyable, not a drudgery. We will have fun – most of the time. I try to get over to my children that when they come into the classroom, they are actually entering France or Germany; I conduct my lessons in the foreign language as far as possible. I hope I convey that there is pleasure and fun in language learning and you do not need to justify French or German in terms of something else. You learn a tremendous number of skills – such as listening, reading, writing and speaking – in learning a language. These skills are character building. You help people to be whole people – they can develop a sense of humour, sensitivity and empathy. There wasn't much scope, it seems to me, for humour and imagination in the 'O'level syllabus, but the GCSE has changed all that.

What I like about GCSE is that there is a lot of room for role-playing. I ask someone to come to the front and mime something, such as the washing-up. Two teams are timed as to how long it takes them to guess what the person is doing. This goes down very well. So many kids wander about the school looking miserable and they come into my class and ask why I've always got a smile on my face. Immediately there's an opportunity to say, 'Well, life is here to be enjoyed!' It is important that as Christian teachers we are able to convey that to our pupils through our teaching as well as through our lives because God wants us to enjoy his creation (1 Tim 6:17).

French teaching can be made much more fun and imaginative than is often thought. For example, there is a section in the GCSE that is called 'personal identification'. This involves details about yourself, your family, your home, your hobbies, your pets. This could be done in a very dry and academic fashion, with lists of words to memorise for homework. The way I chose to do this was to do some listening to start with so as to get the necessary vocabulary. But then, so as to make it really tangible, useful and enjoyable, I sent my pupils away to record all these details on a taperecorder. Then I arranged to do a 'computer-dating' with a friend's school. We both had a fourth-year German class so we arranged to send 'letters' by cassette between the two classes. We exchanged the cassettes and suddenly all the children were really motivated to learn. They even wanted photos! They loved it and their parents were delighted that their kids were so excited. They had never seen them rushing into their rooms to do their homework!

Mark: I appreciate the way you are integrating the aesthetic aspect of creation into your teaching and getting a very good response from your children.

Dave: Another idea that I have found very successful in GCSE is the intruder! It's enjoyable and down to earth. It's also about personal identification – describing people, clothes, colours, etc. You arrange for another teacher to come into the room in really outrageous clothes and waving a gun. There's a hold-up and everyone sticks up their hands. 'The robber' then steals something from someone's bag and leaves. It's best if you could get someone like the deputy head to do it. As soon as the person has gone, you organise the class into little groups to get together in the foreign language a description of the robber for the police. At the end of the lesson you ask the person to come back and you then check which group produced the best description.

Mark: This is great stuff! Now, you have criticised both the traditional and GCSE approaches. On a positive note, what is it about the GCSE that you like?

Dave: What is good about it is the emphasis upon communication rather than accuracy. 'O' level was accessible to a minority but GCSE is much more accessible. It's now possible to get a 'C' with a minimal ability to write French. It encourages imagination and innovation in teaching in a way that 'O' level never did. The possibilities for your teaching are much richer and therefore I believe that languages can be taught in a way which reflects more of the richness and fun of this aspect of God's creation.

CHAPTER FIFTEEN

GEOGRAPHY

Ross has been teaching geography in a comprehensive school for many years. He has thought through his responsibilities very thoroughly and has clearly had some success in presenting a Christian approach to his subject in the context of a comprehensive school. Of particular interest is the way Ross relates the issue of worldview to the environment – different worldviews impact the environment in very different ways. He writes the following.

How do we teach geography from a Christian perspective? It was certainly not part of the syllabus of my university geography course, yet it was at university that I first became aware of what can be described as a Christian approach to geography and with it the challenge to investigate this further.

It came through an article, made available in the vestry of a church I once attended. For me it was one of those 'Ah!' articles which induce a fundamental change in the reader's consciousness, enabling you to see familiar things as though you are seeing and understanding them for the first time.

As Christian teachers, and as Christian geography teachers in particular, we have a tremendous opportunity to open the eyes of our students to the coherence and inter-relationships of the world around them and to instil in them a sense of responsibility for the wise use of these resources; be they renewable ones such as forests, or non-renewable ones such as mineral wealth.

I looked forward to teaching geography but this was soon strained by the early pressures associated with teaching and then by the endless curriculum/examination changes. Nothing seemed to last for long and trying to think from a Christian perspective seemed a luxury. It may well be that with the establishment of GCSE we will enter a more settled period, and the time may be right to find a suitable syllabus within which to develop a more Christian approach.

As a geography teacher I begin with the assumption that this world belongs to God, not to humanity. It is after all his creation – the climatic and vegetation zones, mountains and valleys, foodstuffs and mineral deposits; even 'our' latest acquisition, North Sea oil! So as we teach, what sort of picture do we present of man as God's steward fulfilling his mandate to subdue the earth? Does he do this obediently or disobediently?

That then is my starting point. So what next? We need to teach about people and places but with the emphasis on the interaction between human beings and the natural world. In their activities human beings use and adapt to the natural environment and at the same time they modify and transform that setting. Such an emphasis leads us to concentrate on man and ecological lifestyle.

However, a purely descriptive approach is not enough as we must teach our students that they have a responsibility to take care of the earth. To start with, this can be done by showing examples of how societies have adapted in their environmental setting. This then raises further questions. Why do societies act in such different ways in their response to the environment? Why have some 'desert' countries remained virtually unchanged over centuries, yet others have been able to make the desert bloom in a relatively short time? Is it just a question of technology and wealth?

What is our view of resource management? Why are we seemingly more concerned at the loss of rain forest with its attendant soil exposure, erosion and depletion of the flora and fauna, than those countries where it is happening? How important is it to maintain 'Green Belt' land around our cities if it pushes up the price of houses so that only the wealthier people can afford to purchase the houses that are built? What is more important, people or the environment? Or is this a false dilemma?

To try to answer these questions takes us into the area of values and more significantly brings us up against 'worldviews' or 'heart values'. These are religious statements, an indication of our religious direction. These 'values' are manifested in 'culture', and that culture is at the same time a responding to and modifying of the environment.

These complex inter-relationships are revealed in the varying responses that we notice in different countries. Capitalist and communist systems are different in some ways, and both are different from Islamic, Buddhist or Shinto societies. These differing 'systems' operate in countries that can generally be subdivided again under the basic economic categories of 'Developed', 'Developing' and 'Undeveloped' (those with virtually no known 'exploitable' resources). Finally these religious and economic systems are being developed at a particular place on the earth's surface, within different parts of our ecosystem.

Given such a diversity, we have to choose what we will present to our students in order to give them a broad picture of the world in which they live. Choosing within a framework enables us to introduce variety. For example:

Worldview	Economic status	Politic status	Example
Roman Catholic	Developing	Capitalist	Brazil (Rain Forest)
Post Shinto	Developed	Capitalist	Japan
Islam	Developed	Capitalist	Saudi Arabia

Islam	Undeveloped		Mali (Desert)
Jewish	Developed	Capitalist	Israel
Hindu	Developed/ing?	Capitalist	India
Communist	Developed		USSR
Humanist (Post Christian)	Developed	Capitalist	UK

Yet variety for the sake of it is of no real value. As Christian teachers we are concerned to help our students understand the world they live in. They need to grasp that a nation or culture is always responding either obediently or disobediently to God. We must help them to understand the nature of our own society, so that they can weigh up the implications of social, political and economic decisions. Our consumer society demands food at the lowest price possible. But further development of monoculture in many developing countries to produce coffee or tea, obtained by us at the cheapest price and as part of complex trade deals or aid packages, may be 'good' for us but in the longer term can be disastrous for the producer country.

Our understanding of our own society deepens when we begin to understand others, particularly when we see that other countries act in different ways because of different worldviews.

The BBC series on Japan (made for schools) generates a considerable response each time I show it. It begins with life in the city of Tokyo, moves on to the countryside, and then considers the implications of industrialisation that is moving too fast, the pull of the city, and the consequent depopulation of the countryside. At the same time the series highlights the conflicts between the younger and older generations; traditional values are pressured and replaced by 'western' ones. Such a series enables the Christian teacher to open up the fascinating theme of worldviews and the impact they have upon people's lives and the environment. It is then possible to contrast such worldviews with the one that dominates British society.

The relevance of such an approach can be demonstrated by a topical issue. At the time of writing, differences of opinion have arisen between the governments of the UK and Canada. A proposal has been made here in the UK that furs caught in the wild by certain types of traps should be marked in a special way. It is hoped that such legislation will deter this practice and by a proposal that is without cost to the UK. What are the implications of such legislation for Canadians and in particular the Inuit people?

The Canadian spokesman pointed out that 100,000 people are involved; over half of them live in isolated areas and such a move may well 'affect their culture and the closeness to the land that they enjoy', and might even force them to move away. This example could open up the debate from a Christian perspective as we consider the concept of stewardship. How do Canadian and Inuit peoples use the land and how does this relate to their conflicting worldviews?

So where do we start? Our world is fascinating; virtually everyone would love to travel the world. The pictures in the *National Geographic* magazine have universal appeal. Yet in the classroom we have managed to reduce such rich variety to a bland uniformity, and much of the material we have used has not helped. Could there not be room here from a Christian perspective to teach the subject in a way that does it justice and that challenges students to see that their fundamental calling is to serve Almighty God and that they will do that in their day-by-day cultural activities, either in obedience or in disobedience?

Within the subject we must affirm that God made the world, called it good and directs its course. We believe that God continues to care for the world. When we affirm that God loved the world and that Christ gave his life for the world, we are not just speaking of humanity but the entire created universe. We all know about the greed and evil that seems to be turning the world towards destruction, but we also understand the scope of redemption in Christ and the peacemaking and concern for our planet that the gospel should bring.

CHAPTER SIXTEEN

ENGLISH LITERATURE

George has been teaching RE and English in secondary schools. As he considers English literature, he places upon teachers and parents the responsibility of making decisions about which books to make easily available for young people to read. He gives some very helpful and practical advice about the selection of books reflecting a Christian worldview which will encourage our children's moral and spiritual development.

Everyone, I guess, would agree that one thing schools should do is encourage children to read. I leave to one side the growing importance of the visual media: that is another subject. Here I am concerned with books. Schools are engaged in the task first of teaching children how to read, and secondly in encouraging them to use the reading ability. Basically people read for two purposes – information and pleasure. The two are closely intertwined. As I write these words in a railway carriage, all but one of the ten people sharing it are reading. Their reading matter varies from tabloid newspapers to what could well be a university level textbook, taking in on the way a couple of 'leisure and hobbies' magazines. You can see the wide range of magazine literature in any local branch of the chain newsagents. Not everything they sell is the kind of thing we want our children to read. What, then, can schools do about books, especially books for pleasure? And what can parents do to help their own children?

As a parent and secondary-school teacher I discovered one basic fact. Once they have mastered the actual techniques of reading, children will usually read what is most easily available. Some children will need a good deal of encouragement to learn to enjoy reading at all, others from an early age will eagerly devour everything that comes their way. But for the most part they will all at least begin by reading what is there; what they can get hold of without undue effort. The books which are actually in the classroom, and the books and magazines they find at home – these are the ones they will pick up and read.

As a secondary teacher of RE and English, I ran two class libraries – nothing vast or elaborate; just a couple of shelves each in cupboards. Both reflected some of my own leisure reading. One consisted of science fiction, the other of fairly light Christian literature, mainly biographical, the sort of thing written by Nicky Cruz or Jackie Pullinger, with a sprinkling of books about Christian doctrine and such topics as prayer. I would mention new additions to classes from time to time. Boys (it was a single sex school) could borrow any book freely as long as they signed for it. Not surprisingly, my own fifth year form, in and out of the room every day, made most use of this facility. At the end of one school year I asked them to list the books they'd read for pleasure. To my surprise books in the class library appeared in almost all of the lists. My ordinary class of not-specially-Christian teenagers averaged a higher consumption of Christian books than many a committed Christian adult. They had read, and with evident enjoyment, what was made easily accessible to them.

The experience confirmed what my wife and I found to be the case with our two daughters. We never banned books, we just ensured that the house was as full as we could make it with good wholesome children's literature. No doubt we were fortunate, compared with earlier generations, in bringing our children up in the sixties and early seventies, when a steady flow of fine children's stories was appearing year by year from authors like Rosemary Sutcliff, Hester Burton, Philip Turner, and many others. What couldn't be bought in paperback form could usually be borrowed from the public library. They enjoyed what had been made available – and came back for more.

In the early 1970s one Schools Council research project investigated children's leisure reading, especially story books. The researchers discovered the abiding popularity of the 'children's classics': *Treasure Island, Black Beauty, Little Women*, etc. I am sure that this popularity is due in part to the simple fact that you can buy the books, in a variety of editions, cheaply, in the corner newsagent or the town-centre chain store.

Children, then, will read what is easily available. It is part of our task as teachers and parents to ensure that what is available is good. As Christians we cannot escape a moral and spiritual challenge: what kind of books do we set before the children in our care? We have to start by recognising that fiction, of whatever kind, conveys messages on the moral and spiritual level which are based on a worldview, whether Christian or otherwise. Whether the author is deliberately trying to express a point of view, or simply tell a story, his writing paints a picture of life. Who are the heroes and who are the villains? What kinds of action are held up for approval or disapproval? What values does the author affirm?

In choosing books for our own children and books for the school or class library in the junior and middle years, say up to about age thirteen (second year secondary), I would suggest we select stories which uphold and affirm such qualities as courage, honesty, resourcefulness, friendship, loving family relationships, loyalty, care and respect for other people.

There is much wholesome literature available which stands

for such values. As Christians we might also like to see a recognition of the reality of the spiritual realm and a straightforward presentation of Christian truths within the story context. Realistically, however, we have to accept that in our present secular age it is exceptionally difficult to speak of Christian beliefs in a story in a way which is natural and acceptable to the young reader. Among the many fine writers for children in the past forty years I would single out C S Lewis, Patricia St John and the American writer Madeleine L'Engle as three whose Christianity is explicit in their stories without seeming false or somehow 'tacked on'. There are other children's writers whose Christian faith is as real as those cited, but who do not seek to express it directly in their books.

Looking for 'wholesome' children's literature does not mean providing children with a diet of sugary, sentimental unreality. Good stories for children can be strong meat. C S Lewis' Narnia Chronicles, or Ann Holm's *I am David* do not dismiss or play down the reality of evil. But I would suggest that an important element in most children's literature, which reflects ultimately a Christian view of the universe, is that the story ends with a resolution in favour of goodness. Maybe there is not always a 'happy ending', but there is at the very least an ending which looks forward in hope.

When it comes to children's books, teachers and parents are to a very large extent responsible for what is actually available in the house or the school. There is an abundance of well-written wholesome fare which can be easily obtained. But we do have to be on our guard. Some books now being written for children are definitely not wholesome. There are books which encourage an unhealthy interest in the occult, others which seem to delight in descriptions of violence and cruelty, and still more with sexually explicit scenes. Nihilism and pessimism about life in a meaningless universe, which are features of much modern mainstream literature, appear to be creeping into some books written for children. No doubt they are legitimate expressions of an honestly held philosophy. We need, however, to recognise them for what they are – expressions of a profoundly anti-Christian philosophy. When we understand this we are equipped to decide whether we want our young children to be exposed to such material.

I have said enough to make my point. It matters what books children read for pleasure. They all convey values based on some particular view of life, and while one storybook will rarely affect a child's moral or spiritual attitude deeply, a diet of them over a period of years will certainly have its influence. If there is little good modern children's literature which is openly and explicitly presenting Christianity, there is a great deal which effectively upholds moral and personal values which Christians share. But there is a growing need for discrimination in choosing children's books.

I conclude with four comments drawn from my personal experience.

First, it is best to read for yourself anything you place before children. Make your own checklist of the values and attitudes the book is presenting, then you will have a clearer idea of whether or not you want children to read it.

Secondly, in real life children encounter sadness, loss, bullying, fear, bad language and a host of other experiences from which we might wish to shelter them. Books can actually help them to cope with the realities by presenting them at a distance, as it were. What is important is the way in which the book treats these matters.

Thirdly, the best children's fantasy writing (eg, C S Lewis, George MacDonald, Elizabeth Goudge's *The Little White Horse*, Lloyd Alexander, Ursula Le Guin and Madeleine L'Engle) helps many children, in an age of secularism, to keep open a door of wonder and imagination, an awareness of dimensions beyond everyday routines, which will for some of them be a way in to Christian faith. George MacDonald's *Phantastes* had a profound influence on the young C S Lewis, as told by Lewis in his spiritual autobiography *Surprised by Joy*.

Fourthly, CARE Trust (53 Romney Street, London SW1P 3RF) have produced a book list of Recommended Children's Reading, costing 25p. Christians in Education (16 Maid's Causeway, Cambridge CB5 8DA) operate a system enabling the purchase of recommended books by post.

Anyone wanting to explore the field more fully will find that Pat Wynnejones' book *Pictures on the Page* (Lion) is an excellent Christian introduction to the field of children's literature.

CHAPTER SEVENTEEN

ECONOMICS

Alan, who lives in London, has taught economics at 'A level. He is deeply critical of the dominant approach to the subject, believing that a materialistic worldview is transmitted by the textbooks. He argues that, as Christians, we must rethink the foundations of economics; people are not 'egocentric calculating machines', they are stewards called to love and serve their neighbours. Alan shows how Christian wisdom about 'domestic economics' and 'work direction' can be developed in the classroom.

Mark: Alan, you've taught economics at 'A' level. What were some of your impressions of the normal way it was taught?

Alan: Well, there were two main papers in the syllabus that I taught. One was social and economic history and the other one was economic theory. Let's focus on economic theory. The first thing that worried me a great deal was that you were expected to teach the course and the students would come out at the end of it knowing the answers. But some of them would then go to university and find that the economists stressed that they disagreed with one another because they had different perspectives and value systems. So the 'A' level course was actually giving the illusion that the answers were simply there and that there was general agreement about this.

For example, in the multiple choice paper there were fifty questions. I could identify ten to twenty of them as wrong in the sense that the assumptions they were making were highly dubious. So it was a very dogmatic and doctrinaire approach. The dogmatism that lurked behind the exam papers and the syllabus was a strong commitment to neoclassical economics. This meant that anything radical, be it Christian, socialist or Marxist, was simply ruled out. This neoclassical perspective simply sets up a system of calculations by which you can describe the way in which consumers behave, the way in which firms behave and the way in which the economy copes with stresses and changes that occur.

Mark: Would you say that only one approach to economics is conveyed in the textbooks?

Alan: Yes. For instance, in the macro economics it was a kind of Hicksian version of Keynes, which at that time was already being strongly criticised. First of all it was distorting Keynes' position, and secondly it was actually a position that had a tremendous number of problems itself.[1]

Mark: I've been looking at some economics textbooks. One of the most striking things I've noticed is the assumption that all people have unlimited wants. This theme is expressed in all the economics textbooks that I have examined. Now what kind of impact do you think that is having on young people? What way of seeing the world is that indoctrinating them into?

Alan: 'A' level economics often leads people into business studies where you are taught that you just maximise, especially profits and consumption, and so treat everybody as egocentric calculating machines. This approach is based on the understanding that this is 'positive economics'. You get rid of all norms and values because you are not studying what ought to be the case but what is the case – this is what economics is supposed to do scientifically. People, then, are selfish calculating machines, and if this isn't the case then they jolly well ought to be!

Mark: One of the things I have tried to bring out in this book is that the dominant way we teach children tends to deaden them to issues like justice, stewardship, wisdom and social concern. Such issues cannot really mean anything in the framework of this neoclassical economic theory. Do you think that the way we teach economics deadens young people to the biblical worldview?

Alan: Yes. It is very interesting to notice the difference between the economic theory course and the social and economic history course. In the latter you have to touch people's lives. You deal with unionisation, the problems of poverty in the nineteenth century, the changing patterns of family participation in the economy, the welfare state and a whole range of similar issues. But when you come to economic theory, these issues of life have to be excluded! Now what we see here is the idea of economics as some kind of self-contained science or discipline, the heart of which concerns various ways of calculating. Of course this completely misses out what real economic living is and that is really serious!

Mark: We could say that this approach is very reductionist. As a Christian, how do you go about challenging this? How would you begin to do something about that in the classroom? What kind of concepts would you develop at 'A' level?

Alan: There is a whole range of areas which are very important to people's lives economically. I've become very interested in the idea of the domestic economy. We live together in families, and in families people don't buy and sell things, they give things. We give time, share resources and so on. But at the same time we make hundreds of important economic decisions a day in our family. What will we eat? How will we spend our money? Do I spend time with the family or my mates at the snooker club? Obviously this puts some members of the family under pressure and others under no stress at all. Some families are weak in economic resources and others have a great deal. It is interesting that two-career families very often don't have time to spend their money properly or efficiently. All these are interesting and important issues and I think that everybody needs some awareness of their domestic economy. This kind of teaching can positively increase sensitivity, justice and stewardship within families.

Mark: So what you're doing is dealing with the whole context. You take a group of people in complicated relationships, such as the family, and develop the economics from this. That is very different from the way economics is normally taught. Could you bring out some of the differences between the way you teach and the way you think it's normally done?

Alan: First, let me give you another example. Take work, which is obviously a central economic activity. People are very much bound up in their work so the fact that you train for fifteen years or so means that there is faith vested in a vocational work direction. That is why the idea that relative rates of pay can sort out the labour market is completely false. Basically if you have been training for fifteen years you can't suddenly go for a job that pays a bit more if you aren't qualified for it. We are all precommitted in all kinds of ways when it comes to vocation. Work, then, has a central faith direction and has all kinds of values built into it. It is either egocentric in its reference point – 'my work is my career, it's me making good' – or an act of service. Whether you are talking about the domestic economy or work, you're first of all talking about the kinds of commitments that are basic to the way we live. You are talking about your religious faith, your worldview. Do you adopt a humanist, self-worshipping approach to economics either in your consumption or your work, or do you adopt biblical norms of service, justice and faith?

That's the first issue. The second issue is that people actually vary a great deal in their valuations and these valuations spring from their deeper religious values. I am always amused by what different people see as essential to their lifestyle. Some people will spend hundreds of pounds on a hifi system that will detect the tiniest speck of dust and won't consider that to be extravagant, whereas for others that would be wildly extravagant. However, those other people will spend extravagantly in some other area. In terms of 'valuation', it is very interesting that neoclassical economics has got rid of the theory of value from price theory, and prices are supposed to give values. I think a whole range of work needs to be done to re-establish an understanding of value and the impact that it has on our pricing system.

Mark: So do you think that the normal way that economics is taught very much encourages children to value things in monetary ways?

Alan: Yes. I think that on the whole people are taught that money is the standard of value, so implicitly we are being taught materialism. Nevertheless, the way they actually have to live is to construct their own values. Although people may say that they're going to go after the money and so on, very few are thoroughgoing materialists – the value system they have to live with is so much richer than that. The question of valuation is not discussed within their school curriculum, so it's what they do after school with their mates or elsewhere that supplies them with their valuational judgements.

Note

1. Keynes is one of the most influential economists of the twentieth century. Hicks is a famous economist who has been influenced by Keynes.

CHAPTER EIGHTEEN

SPECIALISM IN SECONDARY SCHOOLS

Charles Martin, who has recently retired from being the Chairman of the Association of Christian Teachers, shares with us how he has challenged what he calls the tyranny of 'specialism'. Are rigidly defined subjects taught by specialists the only valid areas of learning? He sees specialism as an aspect of education which militates against the concept of coherence in Christ, which was discussed in the first section of this book. Charles draws upon his extensive experience and shows how it is possible to change the perceived priorities in schools so that teachers and pupils are given a clearer understanding of goals in education which are more appropriate to a Christian perspective of life and education.

Specialism is the key problem of the secondary curriculum. We can't live without it. We can't live with it. We put up with it for four reasons: 1. We inherited it. 2. There is steady pressure from universities and tradition to keep it. 3. We haven't been able to market an alternative strong enough to get parents (and some governors and teachers) off the specialist drug. 4. It has spawned a mythology among teachers about its own necessity.

  1. Post-1945 grammar schools copied the structure of the

independent schools – a single-subject examination-centred curriculum. The independent schools (especially boarding) had very strong traditions of 'hidden curriculum' which unified staff and pupils and offset the effects of specialism. Grammar schools managed a pale reflection of this in 'school spirit'. Secondary modern schools aped grammar schools instead of striking out boldly to provide for their own clientele. With even less reason than the grammar schools they swallowed the specialist structure. When comprehensive reorganisation swept away the selective system everybody was expecting things to be structured along single-subject, specialist lines.

2. Universities have exercised an uncanny influence. Although they have no interest whatever in 80% of the pupil population, they have dominated discussion of 'A' levels, to which the GCSE exam is firmly linked. So pupils who have no intention whatever of taking 'A' levels have followed GCSE courses narrowly concentrated round one subject area.

3. 'General Studies' got a strong boost in the 1960s when independent school heads said how important it was. Many of them did something about it. Some grammar schools introduced general studies courses in the sixth form. Some tried hard, but were faced with a staff and pupil attitude which had no time for anything except 'proper subjects'. Many comprehensives started off with good integrated Humanities courses in the first and second years. But by the third year they were mostly back to single subjects to prepare pupils for the real world of fourth and fifth year examination study.

Most of the powerful and vocal parents come from grammar schools and remember the specialist teaching – often very good – that they received. They had little else, so don't relate easily to anything they hear from their children or school staff about non-specialist lessons. English was English; Chemistry was Chemistry. This new stuff seems to be all chat about life in general. Gets you nowhere.

4. One of the best mathematics teachers I ever knew was a

history graduate who had got hooked on maths and made it his speciality. He learnt on the job. He took 'A' level maths himself (and got grade A) before going on to teach 'A' level maths. That is unusual. Most heads and governors expect specialist training to be the key factor in appointments. Teachers, they believe, are first and foremost geographers, or scientists or some other specialist. They will also, we hope, be able to help with games, take a tutor group and perhaps put in their two penn'orth to the general studies programme.

That's how more than half the profession sees it too. In primary schools teachers are supposed to know everything. Pupils have one teacher most of the time. In secondary they have eight or more specialists. This break in structure shows four serious outcomes of the myth of specialism. Firstly, the pupil changes from being a 'whole' person to being a kaleidoscope changing seven times a day to fit the content and teaching style of seven specialists. (Have you ever followed a second year pupil round classes for a week to see the incredible adaptability needed?)

Secondly, primary school teachers are downgraded and few secondary teachers have the humility to learn from them.

Thirdly, knowledge, instead of being a robust plant with lots of healthy growing points, is split up like prepacked items collected in a supermarket trolley.

Fourthly, pupils may even leave school without understanding the connectedness of knowledge. Why did they have to wait till sixth form general studies to learn that presuppositions underlie all language and learning; that the fancied 'fact/opinion' dichotomy between science and humanities is a gross error?

This situation, however, is slowly changing and people are being appointed as year heads, pastoral heads and team leaders of cross-curricular teaching groups irrespective of their degree subject. Schools will continue to need a few specialists who know their subject really well, but they will be pathfinders or team leaders, or specialist contributors to a more general team. The specialist barons of the big departments are slowly giving way in power structures to staff whose main interest is the whole development of pupils, academic, personal and social, across the board. But the mythology dies hard. If you have a PhD in zoology you may well be much more highly regarded (and even think yourself better) than a mere BEd who did 'general subjects' even if she teaches those general subjects superbly.

Against that historical background I offer a few notes of how I learnt to live with specialism and stay human. To stay, too, a follower of Christ in whom all things cohere and in whom there is no division.

I was fortunate to work in a large comprehensive school (1,700 pupils) where I learnt the great lesson of staff teamwork. Specialism ruins this, dividing staffrooms into small cliques, at worst fighting for their own department, and at best having an unofficial pecking order, so that physics is more important than secretarial. I learned that staff from different departments could work in a team, sharing a common goal, growing in mutual respect and understanding, each contributing a specialism to the task. So teachers groups for humanities in the first and second years provided material which included English, religious education, history and geography. Ten to twelve teachers used the prepared material with their own tutor group – or at least a group they saw for between eight and twelve periods a week. I have since seen a similar scheme working well at a much smaller comprehensive (seventy-five pupils in each year) where first years spend a third of their timetable integrated round English and local history and second years a similar amount integrated round science and information technology. As far as I can see this can be accommodated within the National Curriculum provisions of the new Act, though the assessment targets will have to be very carefully incorporated. The team of teachers have gained enormously themselves; pupils are better known to these staff and have formed larger friendship groups among themselves.

The specialist cliquiness of the staffroom is mellowed with people who talk more about pupils than departmental matters.

In the first school I mentioned I was also part of a team preparing and using material for PSE (personal and social education) for third, fourth and fifth years. A good idea, ahead of its time (in 1972 the school was just emerging from the embers of three selective schools). In these lessons pupils were encouraged to explore a wide range of personal and social issues, to discuss and even argue (politely). They found it very hard as the teaching style in most other lessons encouraged no such thing. It was however very good for the staff, who learned how hard real education about real issues can be. I think we were winning in the end.

On moving to be Principal of a sixth form college, I faced the same problem, only (like Nebuchadnezzar's furnace) seven times hotter. Specialism seemed the natural and logical structure. Two-thirds of students were doing 'A' levels and half of these were heading for higher education. Most of the staff were excellent specialists with a fair track record of 'A' level success. A general studies programme limped along with little support from students and not much more from staff. They hoped the new Principal would give it a decent burial. Alas for them (and him) the new Principal tried to revive it. After three years I was able to appoint a Director of general studies – an enthusiast and good administrator who got a good scheme going which gave most students five hours a week of study and recreation which complemented their specialist studies. This still seemed a poor relation and was staffed in the main by people who saw their main job as specialists in languages, science or whatever. Over the years the system has strengthened and now involves teaching teams responsible for balanced general programmes for groups of a hundred or so students. Team meetings are more fruitful, both in terms of the personal development of individual teachers and also the more student-related concern. 'What do students need to get out of this?' is the question, rather than, 'How do we get this chunk of material across to the students?'

Other successful ventures include Careers and CPVE (Certificate of Prevocational Education).

The Careers department began recruiting staff teams for 'Access' courses – access to higher education or employment. They were timetabled and all students did a six weeks' course. The compulsion was psychologically significant. It said that learning how to live after school was as important as examination success. Courses covered the usual personal and social issues – self-awareness and appraisal, job appraisal, application and interview technique, decision making, communication (saying and listening), dealing with controversy. For many staff this was new country, but whatever their specialism they learned quickly and gained confidence. Over a few years they rose in staffroom status from cranks with this thing about careers to respected colleagues with an enviable rapport with students.

The CPVE was even more startling. A volunteer team took it on with panache and then found out what a hard job they had started. Not only is the material totally integrated around vocational topics but the assessment is continuous and also negotiated with the student. Most of the customers had had a poor experience of education, and so thought they were failures. No wonder staff needed regular group meetings to reinforce each other and decide the way ahead. From the students' point of view the course was a great success. Forty-six out of fifty-four found employment or college entrance. From the staff point of view the development was phenomenal. They were seeing students grow in confidence and skill as they had never seen it before. They learned to respect the pupils' self-assessment and to be open to question and criticism. They saw students as people, not dependent upon specialist knowledge or skills, and so they became valuable salt and light in the staffroom and the specialist departments in which they served. Specialist teaching still goes on, 60% of the time for the three-'A' level student. 'Results' are still good. In some specialisms teaching styles have changed, being more student-related and less didactic. But specialism is no longer a tyrant. The pecking order has almost gone. General education, pastoral responsibility and specialist teaching are all part of one institution serving the students.

In many comprehensive secondary schools similar thinking is at work. 'Modular' courses give pupils a much wider experience and less of the narrow two-year journey to the vague distant goal of a specialist examination. Technology is also coming to our aid. If more pupils used word-processors in all 'subjects', spelling and grammar correction would be easier (and might even be fun). The final product would not be a laboured rewrite alongside the red-inked first attempt. Would Locospell permanently damage pupils' spelling? It might well do just the reverse. I am not sure if staff integration proceeds with equal pace. I hope so. Staff team meetings need a great investment in time but they can pay huge dividends.

From all this it will be clear that I learned to live with specialism and temper some of its more arrogant features. I haven't cracked it – and won't now since, unlike the House of Lords, schools regard people as 'past it' at sixty-five. But I have been fortunate to live through a period when the whole rationale of the curriculum has been under steady scrutiny. For a very few purposes we still need some (at most 20%) students to have detailed knowledge of a subject area. We have at last begun to realise that this is not all – not even the main job – that schools have to do to prepare young people to become citizens of a humane democracy. The other goals are becoming a little clearer: skills like finding out for yourself, learning to learn, co-operating and working as a member of a team, and tackling problems and applying knowledge rather than just adding to it. We need to foster attitudes like readiness to listen and to weigh what we hear; like respect for other people because of what they are rather than what they know. We must learn to recognise concepts and models that appear in a wide range of 'subjects'. We haven't yet found ways of assessing these desirable qualities. Until we do, specialist single-subject examination grades will rule the roost and employers will go on asking for five GCSEs or two 'A' levels (no matter what) just because they think it 'sorts out the good 'uns'. And for many people, the serious education that goes on in primary schools will be just the prelude to the 'real study' of 'subjects' taught by the super-race of 'specialists'.

CHAPTER NINETEEN

TEAM-TEACHING AND DISCIPLINE

John, who teaches in Suffolk, has been teaching Latin, Italian and RE for many years. He has some observations about discipline, 'team-teaching' and encouraging children to learn from each other, as a result of his own study of the Bible. If corporal punishment had not been abolished under the 1986 Education Act, then John's comments about discipline would have led us into a discussion about corporal punishment. However, I have included his observations about discipline, not to raise that issue, but rather to highlight the problems some teachers have to face and emphasise the need for local churches to give prayerful support to the teachers in their congregations. John's other comments provide some interesting thoughts on crucial issues related to the way curriculum subjects are taught.

Education observations

I have been in education – secondary, tertiary and adult – for most of my working life. Some fifteen years ago I began to tackle seriously the question of a distinctively Christian approach to education. I found that the result was unique, not in its separate ingredients, but in its particular 'mix' of those ingredients.

I have been, by nature, strongly averse to the use of corporal punishment, and until fairly recently I have had little trouble in keeping discipline. On the principle which is implied in both the record of Scripture and in the very fact of its existence, I always made a policy of spelling out clearly to the children the terms on which I expected to run a class, and this has (until quite recently) always been respected, if not always observed!

Up to three years ago, I can only recall one occasion when corporal punishment was necessary. It was in a case where a boy openly challenged my authority. It was extremely distressing to me and gave me a disturbing sense of failure. Yet it established my position, and seemed to claim respect. Curiously enough, after he left school, the boy visited me at home to tell me how he was getting on (no mention was made of the incident, or even suggested); he was in fact the only one from that particular class I can recall doing that.

In more recent years, discipline problems have become increasingly difficult; the processes of report, detention and notifying parents seem to be largely ineffective. It seems to me that the problems of discipline are becoming the most significant factor in poor teaching morale. Unless one has been in a classroom situation it is difficult to imagine the strain imposed by one 'bad' lesson; it can cloud the whole day and even the whole week. None of the devices I have seen teachers adopt deal with this problem in a satisfactory way.

I have often been fascinated by Matthew chapter 10. Here is a teacher offering a revolutionary approach to life, sending out as his representatives people who had no rabbinic qualifications and only a few months' informal instruction.

It took some reflection to realise that my best teaching tends to be done when I have just mastered a subject myself, and the difficulties are still fresh in my mind. In other words, education is best done by the brighter pupils teaching the less bright. However, the normal approach tends to sit the pupils in rows, carefully facing one way. We test them competitively and we are uneasy about collaboration in homework.

But think of the advantages of schooling where the better pupils teach the rest. The brighter ones are no longer bored by having to wait for the rest; they enjoy a sense of achievement in being able to use their new knowledge. Pupils learn knowing that what they learn will be immediately used. Competition in knowledge is replaced by collaboration.

Furthermore, it is a commonplace that you have only really mastered a subject properly when you are able to explain it to others. This would help to weaken the tendency to élitism among the academically bright. Schools would not only be producing people who know, but people who can teach. We will be developing a society in which standards of teaching and explanation are raised for almost everybody with the result that professionally trained teaching will reach a very high level indeed. The teacher would spend less time and energy exclusively on less able children – and indeed on coping with a wide range of abilities; this would give greater opportunity for the personal contact which means so much in the classroom. The present system of desk and classroom, with pupils not living in the immediate area of the school, was something I found to be an insuperable obstacle to implementing such a vision, even on a small scale.

My biblical studies have led me to another related idea. Others have reached 'team-teaching' by sheer imaginative trial and error. The biblical insight that it is not good for man to be alone, the pluralism of office in the Old Testament socio-political structure, and the New Testament practice of working in pairs or groups, suggests that the custom of having one teacher in isolation in one class is a recipe for trouble.

At one school where I taught over a period of some seven years, we were eventually induced to try running classes in 'integrated studies' (not a very popular course in itself) with two teachers to a class of some fifty children. Many of those who took part spoke of it as one of the most rewarding experiences of their lives. There were some initial inhibitions; we had never exposed our teaching methods and their weaknesses to anyone since our probationary period. But the advantages were colossal. We lost the burden of isolation when there were problems in the classroom. We found ourselves complementing each other's abilities and weaknesses. When there was a need for one child to have special attention, or to set up equipment, there was still someone to look after the rest. If one fell sick, the other knew exactly where to follow on. And hearing two voices rather than one was an aid to interest and concentration; perhaps even more importantly, it enabled pupils to see two points of view in dialogue, and to experience a healthy sharing of new ideas and accumulated expertise between the newcomers and oldstagers of the profession.

Perhaps the most important discovery that biblical notions of education (especially in the Old Testament) brought to me, was the realisation of what education is really all about. It is often assumed that the Old Testament educational programme was religious in the modern sense of RE, and that it was so because of a primitive and somewhat naïve outlook on life. It is becoming increasingly apparent that all education is an expression of a cultural value-system which ultimately springs from religious root attitudes (in the sense that they are ultimate, axiomatic assumptions made about life and taken on trust – ie, faith).

The ultimate aim of education (and of any teacher in any subject in it) is an understanding of life in the context of that value-system – that is, in terms of its meaning. This is not simply fulfilled when a pupil gains formal knowledge combined with certain skills in manipulating and applying it. The real goal – and every teacher consciously or unconsciously finds fulfilment in seeing it – is insight; the brightening of the face and the gleam in the eye when a student says something like, 'Ah...I see.' If there is no agreed and adequate value-system within which that can take place, the teacher's task becomes a relatively uninspired and uninspiring affair.

CHAPTER TWENTY

AVOIDING INDOCTRINATION

This book has attempted to show that through their curriculum studies children in our schools are being 'indoctrinated' into a secular view of the world because that is portrayed as being neutral and no alternative view is presented. While Christians would want to say that there is an alternative view which provides a much richer, more fulfilling perspective of reality, Christian teachers need to be wary of that same charge of 'indoctrination' in the way they teach.

George has had many years' experience as an RE teacher, as well as being an RE inspector in ILEA. He tackles this issue of the way a committed Christian should teach with guidelines he calls 'Ten Tips for Tightrope Walkers'!

Everyone brings commitments of different kinds into the classroom. As teachers we are all presumably committed in some way to children – there would be cause for concern if we weren't! No doubt we are also committed to the importance of whatever we are teaching – music, literature, maths, etc. We are all, whatever our religious or non-religious beliefs, in some sense committed to a set of values and a way of life.

Suspect any teacher who claims to go into the classroom neutral about such matters. He is either deceiving himself, or attempting to deceive the children, or both. The claim to be a detached, impartial observer of life will not stand up. Even in a school environment we are actually embroiled in the business of living, and our values and commitments will show in the way we set about it – the way we treat one another and our pupils, the way we talk, the things we do, the situations which call forth our anger or our delight, and the ways we express those reactions.

Our values and commitments make us what we are. Encounter with them is part of a child's education. We could not alter this even if we wished to. But in fact there is nothing educationally wrong about our having commitments or expressing them in the classroom. The attempt to conceal or disguise them may be misleading and unhelpful to children. The way we express them may be profoundly wrong and damaging – if, for instance, we are dismissive or prejudiced about other people or their views. The teacher who says, 'Now we've finished with that nonsense [school prayers], let's get on with some really important matters,' is no doubt expressing personal convictions, but in a way totally unacceptable in the classroom (and you don't have to use actual words to convey such a message). In the same way the teacher of religion (very likely a religious teacher) who caricatures or laughs at the beliefs of other people is expressing his or her personal convictions in an equally unacceptable way.

The following 'Ten Tips for Tightrope Walkers' are primarily for the Christian RE teacher but they serve equally as guidelines for all teachers called upon to tackle in the classroom, issues of importance and controversy about which they have strong convictions, beliefs and commitments. They will, if seriously applied, help our pupils to understand and handle other people's commitments. They will give a model for the treatment of differences which will help our pupils to live more fully in a pluralist world. They will enable us, as teachers, to tackle more easily with integrity a task which requires us to do justice to the beliefs and aspirations of our pupils and their families, without compromising our own allegiance to our Lord Jesus Christ. My title itself is, of course, significant. It is actually easier to walk a tightrope than to describe how to do so:

Ten Tips for Tightrope Walkers

1. Be honest – both to yourself and to the children. You have a *right* to be yourself, and a *need* to be seen as what you are. Your pupils have a *right* to see you as you are and a *need* educationally to see what makes you 'tick'.

2. Be fair to views you do not share or agree with. No caricatures. No 'snide' comments. No comparing the best of your faith with the worst of someone else's.

3. When you don't know, admit it, and be prepared (if the matter is important enough) to find out. *Never* fill in the gaps in your knowledge of some other faith by guesswork or approximation.

4. If you slip into error or misrepresentation, apologise and make correction. The genuine apology, without excuses, is becoming so rare a feature of life in our society that when it occurs it will often be a memorable and positive occasion, and you will offer your pupils a model for good behaviour.

5. Where you have a bias on a matter under discussion, it will help your pupils to assess your contribution if you acknowledge it.

6. Distinguish (and help pupils to do so) between matters of fact and matters of opinion (eg matter of fact: Christians believe Jesus is the Son of God; matter of opinion: whether they are right or wrong).

7. Be sensitive and listen with courtesy to children. Take them seriously, especially when they are opening up to you and the class on matters of personal belief or concern. This becomes more difficult, but also more important,

when they are propounding something you personally regard as nonsense. What is at stake here is the creation of an atmosphere of trust in which it becomes possible to share and consider sensitive issues such as prayer or the problem of undeserved suffering.

8. *Never* use your weight as a teacher in argument: 'When you're as old as I am...' and, 'When you've had my experience...' are indefensible discussion gambits. In the teacher/pupil relationship they are far too easily a form of bullying. Use them and you will shatter your own credibility.

9. Keep your temper.

10. Cultivate a sense of humour – especially the ability to laugh at yourself.

I've tried to keep these tips short. I'm aware some of them could provoke all kinds of discussion themselves, but I ask you not to dissect them word by word. They are not intended to be any more than the title suggests, practical tips. If I were to summarise even more drastically I might say:

Be honest

Be courteous

Be sensitive

Love your pupils as yourself

All that I've advocated I have seen as part of my own Christian witness in the classroom. I wish I could claim that I've always applied my own tips fully and completely. Not so! I've worked them out with some pain and anguish, and with a fair share of mistakes along the way. Perhaps it is unnecessary for me to add that I assume the Christian teacher's classroom practice will be backed up by lots of prayer.

CHAPTER TWENTY-ONE

TEACHING AT JUNIOR AND PRIMARY LEVELS

Let us now turn our attention to what is happening within some primary schools.

There is often a very different atmosphere in a primary or junior school than there is in a secondary school. Very often (not always) a primary school can display a warmth and integration that is lacking in the secondary school. Colour, playful exploration and integrated project work can provide a meaningful environment for young children.

Within the primary school it is often the environment and context of education which is most important for the pupils. It not only provides the whole background to the understanding of the curriculum but affects the children's relationships one with another, which is such an important aspect of education at the primary level.

An Anti-Racist Context of Education

Simon is the headmaster of a Church of England primary school in ILEA. He has had to think through, from a biblical perspective, the authority's anti-racist policy and how it should apply to his school. He begins by outlining the biblical teaching relevant to issues of racism.

The Bible teaches us first to love God and then 'our neighbour as ourself' (Lev 19:18). This is expanded in the same chapter as follows: 'The alien living with you must be treated as one of your native born. Love him as yourself.' (v 34). It was to clarify this point that Jesus told the parable of the Good Samaritan in Luke 10:29–37. This is the same Jesus who sent his disciples to baptise 'all nations in the name of the Father and the Son and of the Holy Ghost' (Mat 28:19).

Paul, writing to the Galatians, spells out the radical nature of Christianity, clearly laying down a racial, social and sexual equality, revolutionary in concept then, and still being strived for today. 'For ye are all the children of God by faith in Christ Jesus. For as many of you as have been baptised into Christ have put on Christ. There is neither Jew nor Greek, there is neither bond nor free, there is neither male nor female, for ye are all one in Christ Jesus' (Gal 3:26–28).

Given such clear, specific and unambiguous biblical teaching, it is even more important for church schools to put God's instructions into practice than for those schools who have an anti-racist policy from a humanistic desire to do what is right. ILEA schools have much to thank the authority for in focusing attention on such vital issues, not only in our capital but also across the nation.

It is worth comparing the above Christian doctrine with the opening section of the authority's anti-racist statement:

> The Inner London Education Authority is committed to achieving equality in education and employment in the Inner London education service. This means the development of an education from which racism, sexism and class discrimination and prejudice have been eliminated so that the Authority can respond fully to the needs of our multi-ethnic society. This paper is concerned with one of the three major obstacles to achieving equality – racism.
>
> Many reports, official and unofficial, have indicated clearly the extent and effects of racism in education. The chief victims are

black people, ie, Afro-Caribbean and Asian communities. Other ethnic minorities are also subjected to racial prejudice and discrimination. However, it is in the interests of all our employees, students and pupils that we actively seek to eliminate racism in all our institutions and in all branches of the service.

There is, rightly, among the black communities and other ethnic minorities, an implacable opposition and resistance to racism. This is a powerful and positive factor in British society. Another force is also available to the service. This is the strong tradition in British society of opposition to injustice in whatever shape or form. All employees of ILEA and users of the Authority's service are uniquely placed, if only they would seize their opportunity, to educate generations of young people free of racism and prejudice.

It may be clearly seen that as regards principle, both views coincide completely.

It is perhaps unfortunate that in its statement the authority takes such a narrow and insular view of racism. 'Racist ideology – surrounding attitudes, values and beliefs – is based on the assumption that black people are inferior to white people.'

One of our staff members escaped from a train bound for Belsen: her crime? Being Jewish. Children at our school relate the story of their own family: grandparents killed in a concentration camp; father escaping as a fourteen-year-old boy.

Racist ideology surrounding attitudes, values and beliefs is based on the assumption that one race is inferior to another whether black or white. I am convinced that any group may adopt racist attitudes towards another, as evidenced by the tribal situation in Zimbabwe today, the racial hatred in the Middle East, or the unacceptably inhumane policy of apartheid in South Africa.

Racism is a human trait, stemming from mankind's selfish nature. To ignore such a reality is both naïve and foolish, and we would be less than honest if we failed to admit this. Nevertheless, in practical terms in London today, it is the various 'black' ethnic groups that suffer directly from racism, and it is essential that we make every effort possible to eradicate racism in all its forms from our society.

The 'opposition to injustice' which the authority so rightly refers to in the initial quotation above is strongly held by primary school children. 'It's not fair' is instantly recognised and identified with by all junior children and many infants, who expect a fair system of justice, particularly from school teachers and other staff. It is therefore quite unrealistic and highly counter-productive to present children with situations where the behaviour is not so classified. It is because of the simplistic ease with which children see the concepts of 'fairness' and 'justice' that such emphasis is placed on this particular point. Our prime aim in our anti-racist policy is to achieve equality of opportunity and good relations between persons of different racial groups and to eliminate racial discrimination: not to talk about it; not to write about it; but to achieve it. We must therefore make the policy workable not only for adults, who are aware of the structural, political, ideological, historical and cultural factors influencing our attitudes, but also for young children faced with a here-and-now situation which their egocentric minds can only see as fair and not fair as applied to them.

Given the above philosophy we find two distinct and varying courses of action open to us. First, we can prevent discrimination by positively promoting racial harmony. Secondly, we can take positive action against any racist incidents or expressed attitudes whether verbal, printed or enacted.

Let us start with how we deal with racist incidents.

1. We must ensure that the children are actually aware of what they are saying, explaining the racial nature of their comments. This is particularly important when dealing with younger children who often merely copy the behaviour of others older than themselves, whether adults or older children. One frequently hears 'black' taunts being used not only by white children towards black or black to black but also

black to white where there is no understanding of the meaning of the terminology used.

2. We must apply appropriate sanctions against the perpetrators of racial insults, taunts or forms of violence or exclusion.

3. We must demand that the parents attend the school to discuss the matter, thus re-emphasising the serious nature of such incidents, and underlining our determination to act effectively against racism.

Throughout, our aim is to act in the interest of:

(a) the child guilty of racist behaviour
(b) the child on the receiving end of racism
(c) all other children in the class/group/school concerned for whom it is appropriate that our attitude is clearly expressed.

As in all matters concerning children, the promotion of what is positively good is always more important than just being negative about what is bad. Therefore much effort has been and will continue to be expended to promote the racial harmony our Christian commitment demands of us.

There are many ways open to us to promote such harmony. Below are some of the ways in which we have been attempting to carry out our aims.

1. We draw on the varied cultural backgrounds of the children and their parents whenever appropriate to any activity, and doing so as a natural part of education rather than as special 'cultural' activities. Our particular aim is to emphasise the value of varying cultures, to expect to obtain value from them, and to do so without creating embarrassment or discomfort in the children. As part of such a process we would attempt to promote the children's use of their mother tongues – to demonstrate particularly our approval of such use and our admiration of those who can speak more than just one language.

2. We have been attempting to increase the number of positive images to be found in the materials available to chil-

dren. This is not only of printed material but also jigsaws, dolls, pictures and clothes – but only and specifically when such material is 'good'. It is a gross act of patronising racism to provide poor quality 'ethnic' material when other material is always carefully selected for quality of both content, construction and presentation.

3. An increase in our own knowledge of varying cultures and a heightening of our own awareness of racist activities and attitudes has been an ongoing process over the last couple of years, and continues to develop.

4. We have become most aware that we need, when formulating school policy in any given area, to be acutely conscious of the implications of such a policy for our varying ethnic groups.

5. We have felt that this entire matter has been of such importance as to demand that we take action of a positively discriminatory nature in terms not only of our behaviour but also of our expenditure.

Awe and wonder

Within the primary school there are exciting opportunities for teachers to introduce their pupils to an appreciation of the variety and wonder of God's creation, as the Bible encourages us to do. The following science activity with a glass tank, taking place within a London infants' school, enabled the children to enjoy the diversity of a small part of God's world. The chart related to this project indicates just how far this sense of 'awe and wonder' could then be integrated with other aspects of the school curriculum. Christine explains how the children responded.

At first glance it may appear difficult to see how a child can experience something of the awe and wonder of God by looking into a murky tank full of pond water.

Last year, my class of thirty five- to seven-year-olds would daily come into class and head straight for the little tank, to see if they could spot any new changes that might have taken place overnight. One morning there was a great commotion as they found that the slimy lump of jelly on the side was alive with tiny, perfectly formed baby snails.

The primary reason for putting the tank in the class was to encourage in the children an investigative approach to their surroundings and to show them how to look closely at things using magnifying glasses. I soon found that this was only the tip of the iceberg and in fact a great deal of learning took place which related to all aspects of the curriculum. The 'wheel' diagram that follows shows just some of the scope for this topic.

I was amazed at just how long a five year old would sit and gaze into a little pot observing a snail or water flea with a magnifying glass and then record in detail its movements, colour, shape and size in drawings and writing.

One day a water tiger ate a tadpole in a yoghurt pot. This led to discussions about a food chain and the effects pollution can have on it. It also led to discussion about death and what happens when we die.

One very clear outcome of our study of the water creatures was the sense of awe and wonder it created in the children. We had talked about the creation story as told in the Bible in previous weeks but now the children asked questions like, 'How did God make every creature different?' And made comments such as, 'God must be very clever.'

One prayer a seven year old wrote sums up for me the effect such a study had on his spiritual understanding. It was similar to this: 'Oh God, how can you think and live and move? How can you do all that you do? Oh God, you're great!'

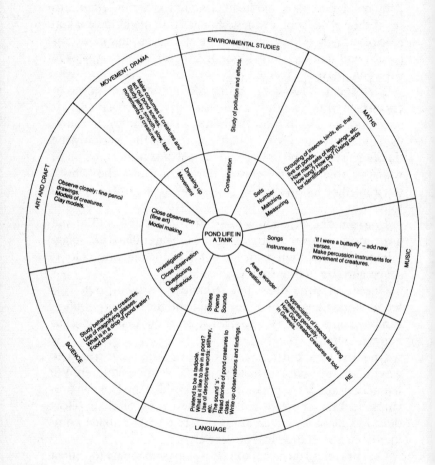

Figure 3

Religious education

Margaret teaches a class of thirty-two six- to seven-year-old children in an infants' school in Cambridge. The theme that she chose for an integrated approach to her children's learning has enabled her not only to familiarise the children with some biblical stories, but show how the characters' experience related to lifestyle and culture. She also uses this context to raise some interesting issues about our need to be good stewards of God's world.

Having just returned from working in Malawi and Sudan I decided on 'Africa' as my theme for the term. I wanted to get away from the usual themes of 'Autumn' and 'Harvest' and 'People who help us'; I longed for the children to learn about something a little more removed from their everyday experiences. By looking at climates, cultures, music, history and countries other than their own, I hoped to give them a much broader view than the 'starving children' picture they are familiar with. I wanted my teaching to reflect a biblical worldview: that God created a world that was good, but the Fall has distorted all of creation and God's call on us is to help restore his broken world. We have made a mess of our world. Forests are cut down causing desertification, erosion of fertile top soil, flooding and famine. We have also made a mess of our relationships. Failure to accept one another has led to discrimination, persecution, mass migrations of refugees and war.

To introduce the particular contribution of RE to my overall theme, I started with the familiar hungry refugee picture and we explored the situation of people on the move, and what it is like to go to a new home, country, school or class. We thought about how we can help in making other people feel welcome. Abraham leaving his home behind for a new country fitted in here. We continued with the Old Testament stories of Isaac and Rebekah, Jacob and Esau, and came to the story of Joseph just in time for harvest celebrations. The stories not only gave much historical and geographical detail to the children, including desert travel, livestock, water supply and nomadic lifestyle, but also explored deep human experiences of jealousy, deceit, rivalry, repentance and forgiveness which the children readily identified with.

The story of Joseph enabled us to explore the culture of some of ancient Africa; the buildings, agriculture, art, religions and alphabet of ancient Egypt. We made Egyptian headdresses and necklaces, and wrote our names in hieroglyphics. A visit to a local museum and an Egyptian day where we dressed and ate Egyptian style made some of Africa's rich past come to life.

Simple irrigation, deforestation and dehydration experiments in the sand and water tray helped to emphasise the need for us to tend and care for our environment, and Joseph's generosity to the Hebrew people was an interesting example of ancient 'food aid'.

As Christmas drew near we left the Old Testament stories, promising to return after Christmas to find out what happened to Joseph's great grandchildren and went on to the nativity story, only to find that Joseph, Mary and Jesus were also refugees in Egypt.

David has been teaching in an independent Christian school for several years, and he is exploring some very exciting possibilities. Being within a Christian school he is more able to draw out some of the explicitly 'Christian' aspects of his project than would be appropriate within a county school. However, any primary or junior school teacher could learn a great deal from him. The age range in his school spans from seven to thirteen. I am particularly interested in the way that Trinity

School integrates history, English, geography, 'worldview', music, poetry, art and drama. The way in which the school's curriculum is touching the Ukrainian community in Britain is also quite remarkable. David explains....

A holistic approach to education

Some years ago I recall asking a student at a university Christian union meeting this question, 'How does your being a Christian affect your approach to town planning?' He thought for a moment before admitting that he had never really supposed that there might be a connection between Christianity and town planning.

This incident illustrates the point that most people view life in bits and pieces. Our educational system, especially at the secondary school level, tends to perpetuate this situation by compartmentalising knowledge into rigidly defined subject areas. There are laudable attempts at integration in some schools, but it is still largely true that the average subject teacher in a comprehensive school knows little about what other teachers are doing in their lessons. When I used to teach RE in a secondary school I knew nothing of what was being taught in other subjects. At the same time it is true that much more integration goes on in primary and junior schools.

Since coming to teach at a Christian school, I have had more opportunity to reflect upon this state of affairs, and to endeavour, together with other teachers here, to bring a greater measure of integration into the curriculum. We still have a long way to go, but at least we are on the way. Before giving some concrete examples of how we have endeavoured to work out a holistic approach to education, I would like to stress three points.

First, Christians have a very special responsibility to encourage integration, because we believe that in Christ all things really do hold together (Col 1:17). Integration and unity in diversity are not just hopeful ideas – they are grounded in the truth about Jesus Christ and what he has done, not just for us, but for all creation.

Secondly, it is vital that all teaching should be conducted with great enthusiasm. The word 'enthusiasm' comes from the Greek *en Theos*: in God, implying the reality of God's energising presence in us. In New Testament times the teachers of the Law (the scribes) were given a key when they started their career, which symbolised authority and the fact that they were to open up the truth to others. This is the context of Jesus' statement in Matthew 13:52: 'Every teacher of the law who has been instructed about the kingdom of heaven is like the owner of a house who brings out of his storeroom new treasures as well as old.' The Christian teacher has the key because 'in Christ are hid all the treasures of wisdom and knowledge' (Col 2:3). So often pupils are bored with the work they do and sometimes this is because the teacher is not especially fascinated and intrigued by the subject matter either. The Christian teacher should be an enthusiast who takes the key, goes to the storeroom and brings out fresh and interesting material. In any project I tackle I learn new and precious things, and the pupils often teach me new things too!

Finally it is vital that we ensure that all we do has meaning for the children as well as for the teachers. Years ago, Solomon saw the emptiness of accumulating fact upon fact. So much of that which passes for education is merely going round and round in a circle of meaninglessness for children, and probably for many teachers as well. If I were to tell a junior pupil that 'in Christ everything holds together' it would probably seem pretty vague and theoretical. But the concept begins to take on meaning as it is made concrete in definite acts of service or praise to the Lord.

At Trinity School we have projects on countries or regions of the world. These run from November to April and involve pupils aged seven to thirteen. The concept of nations and peoples is a very important one in Scripture, beginning with the table of nations in Genesis 10 which, significantly, is placed *before* the Tower of Babel, showing that the diversity of nations is not a result of sin (the confusion of languages is). Paul stresses the divine origin of nations in Acts 17:26 and that their geographical location and history are clearly significant in the context of the Great Commission. Several passages in Revelation indicate that the nations will still be clearly defined in the world to come (eg Rev 5:9, 21:24 and 22:2). We in Britain are notoriously, and perhaps inevitably, insular, but a biblical perception means that we must think globally.

Recently we have completed a major project on the Soviet Union. Here is an outline of some of the aspects of the project.

1. Countries and races in the USSR

For the reasons stated above, this seemed an important place to begin. The impression of the USSR in most people's minds is flat grey monochrome; many people simply call it Russia. Russia is just one (very large!) country within the Soviet Union. We often fail to appreciate that Ukraine is the second largest country in Europe, with a place in the United Nations. How many know that the Chernobyl disaster occurred in Ukraine and not in Russia? Pupils colour in maps of all the different countries of the Soviet Union and make their flags, even getting their tongues round names like Lithuania, Tadzhikstan and Azerbaijan. This really begins to convey the colour and diversity of the USSR! We also show that there are many other people groups in the Soviet Union. Indeed our geographical component, while it does include teaching on major features of the land, weather etc, is generally people centred.

2. History of the USSR

The Cimmerians or Gimeri are thought to be descended from Gomer (Gen 10:2). They were early settlers in the Black Sea region, and Crimea probably derives its name from them. The Scythians are a particularly interesting people, and there are obvious comparisons with the Plains Indians. Other important aspects covered were the coming of Christianity in 988, the Mongol Invasion, famous rulers like Ivan the Terrible, Peter the Great and Catherine the Great, the serfs, and of course the Russian Revolution itself. It is also important to show the huge contribution made by the Soviet Union in the defeat of Hitler.

3. Communism

At Trinity School we feel it is vital that children should learn not just the Christian worldview, but also the major worldviews that influence our world today. The existence of the cotton mills in this area has made it easier for me to explain how Karl Marx formed his ideas. Here is one experiment which will get children to think about communism.

Ask the pupils to bring in their pocket money next week. When the pocket money comes in next week, divide it equally among the class. Now there are several questions to be asked.

(a) What should we do about the people who did not bring their pocket money, or those who refused to share it?

(b) How do the rest of the class feel about the rebels?

(c) How do the rebels feel about the conformists?

(d) Did the teacher act justly or use too much force?

(e) How did those who normally have less pocket money feel about getting more this week?

(f) How did those who normally have more pocket money feel about getting less this week?

(g) Would the class be willing to continue this experiment?

(h) How about taking out, say, a tenth of the total collected to go to some worthy cause (supporting Christians in USSR?) before sharing it out equally again.

(i) Were decisions made by the teacher alone, the teacher and a few 'pets', or co-operatively?

All this needs to be discussed alongside Acts 2:44,45 and 4:32–37.

4. Christianity and other religions in the USSR

There is a wealth of material on this topic. I obtained resources from different organisations and then allocated specific mini-projects to pupils, such as:

(a) Christian children and pressures at school.

(b) Christian youth.

(c) Christians in prison.

(d) Christianity and the law.

(e) The underground printing press.

(f) Music in churches.

(g) Particular people, such as Valeri Barinov.

The pupils produced poster work on their topic and were able to teach the rest of the class about what they had learnt.

5. Music from the USSR

There is endless scope here. Russian classical music often relates to historical events such as Tchaikovsky's '1812 Overture' for Napoleon's retreat from Moscow. I sometimes like to have background music (which relates to the project) while pupils are doing work on their own.

6. Art appreciation

I have found it very useful to use the paintings of Soviet artists to bring history and geography to life. Icons are a particularly important art form, and we have also looked at the rich symbolism of the painted Ukrainian Easter eggs. The paintings of the Itinerants of the late nineteenth and early twentieth century are particularly good for demonstrating the conditions prevailing in the USSR which led to the Revolution.

7. Display work

We produced one very large display (15′ × 8′) called 'Life in the Soviet Union'. The centrepiece was a map of the Soviet

Union. We did the map by tracing round an OHP slide map of the USSR. The map was a major source of information, including many small photographs (from tourist brochures or magazines) or drawings by pupils with appropriate captions. On either side of the map there was poster work about Christians in the Soviet Union. The display also included all the flags of the fifteen republics and some drawings of flowers of the USSR. After the display had been up for a month or so, I devised a quiz on it. It is important that the display should be located where it can be a source of wonder and information for parents and other visitors to the school.

8. Contact with Ukrainians

It is extremely valuable to bring in peoples from the countries being considered. Often this is not as difficult as teachers may first imagine. When we covered Central America, I was able to bring in a Costa Rican and a Salvadorean as well as people who had visited Nicaragua. Through embassies, universities or colleges, it is usually possible to find someone, and often they would be willing to stay overnight if your school is far from a city. I shall never forget the amazement of the Costa Rican on finding that young children knew where his country was and genuinely wanted to find out more!

As far as the Soviet Union is concerned, we soon discovered that there was a significant body of people who had come to Britain from the Soviet Union. There are 35,000 Ukrainians in Britain, many of whom came here soon after the Second World War. The first generation of exiles are particularly interesting for pupils to meet. Most of them were born in the time of Stalin and lived through harrowing experiences, including the forced famine of 1933 and then being used by the Germans in munitions factories or farms in the Second World War. Pupils began to empathise with this significant ethnic minority, many of whom have had little meaningful contact with British people since they arrived more than forty years ago.

1988 has been an especially important year for the Ukrainians because it is the millennium of the coming of Christianity to Kiev (now capital of Ukraine) in 988. The story is a fascinating one and so we produced a play about it entitled 'Kingdom Come in Kiev'. The pupils definitely saw this as the climax of the Soviet Union project. It was not only an opportunity to learn new skills, but a challenge to produce something that, we hoped, would bring the Ukrainians to a clearer understanding of their own history and the gospel. In December 1987 we had two school performances and some Ukrainians came. They appreciated it so much that we were asked to put on performances for Ukrainian communities in Oldham and Ashton in March 1988. Both performances were well attended and it was very moving to receive letters assuring us that the message had been received and accepted. A full page review of the play appeared in a Ukrainian magazine published in Paris for all Ukrainians, and of course it was interesting to see our names in Ukrainian print, but more wonderful to think that our little school could in this unusual way share something of the gospel with thousands. The play is now being translated into Ukrainian.

It is impossible to describe adequately all the elements in a project of this nature. Flexibility is vital. While I plan aspects of a project in advance, many surprising things crop up as we go along. For example, we became very interested in the problems of the Armenians in Azerbaijan, which led to a vast demonstration in Armenia's capital, Yerevan. We discovered that Armenia was the first nation to accept Christianity officially, and as we scratched the surface we realised there was potential for a whole new project and another play.

There is a sense in which each project, while it may borrow useful ideas from elsewhere, should be unique and creative. If you do a project on the Soviet Union, God may well lead you to stress different aspects.

Prayer is another key factor. Teachers should seek God individually and corporately about all that they are going to teach. We have often stopped in the lessons to pray for Christians in the Soviet Union. Before play rehearsals, we would sit in a circle and pray for one another. We saw God put courage into the fearful and what seemed impossible was achieved.

All the pupils' work was recorded in scrapbooks of A4 size. I prefer these to exercise books because they enable everything on the given topic to be kept, as most pupils take great care to produce neat, attractive work with a strong visual appeal. With the Soviet Union project, pupils included tickets, programmes and press cuttings from the play, and they have been able to put in 'extras' if they wish when they find further information on the Soviet Union from brochures or magazines.

This project was not perfect because there were human beings like me involved in it! I failed to involve other staff adequately and there were many 'gaps'. However, our own shortcomings should never prevent us from attempting ambitious and exciting projects in our schools. With the Lord's help it is amazing what can be achieved. Let me close with a favourite scripture which should enthuse and encourage every teacher: 'He will be the sure foundation for your times, a rich store of salvation and wisdom and knowledge; the fear of the Lord is the key to this treasure' (Isa 33:6).

We close this chapter with an example of a Christian primary/junior school where two teachers have been able to give the whole of their school curriculum a specifically biblical perspective.

Ruth is the principal of the school and Jacky teaches science. They have a rather unusual approach to curriculum and their focus is the 'knowledge of God'. I am particularly interested in their attempts at integration and found the project on the redemption of cities fascinating. Parents will find their approach most interesting because it relates the whole context of learning to the development of the children's knowledge of God. Ultimately God gives to parents the responsibility for the education of their children and the privilege of bringing them up to know him. New independent Christian schools are beginning to develop in this country because parents and churches feel that these schools provide the only way that their children's education will reflect their own biblical faith and understanding of the world. Within these schools the whole curriculum can be approached from a Christian perspective. However, most parents have to exercise their responsibility for their children's spiritual growth and awareness while they are being educated within the maintained system of education.

Ruth and Jacky's project not only shows what is possible within a Christian school, but also gives parents an idea of the way 'knowledge of God' can be related to an understanding of the world he has created. They explain:

The focal point of our organisation of teaching material at Oak Hill School is the knowledge of God. Unlike most of the current educational thinking, knowledge in the biblical sense is more than simply intellectual understanding, which in our culture is itself deified; it is always the knowledge of God. Wisdom, or a deep desire to be obedient to God and his principles for life, will teach us to practise and understand God's norms and values and this in turn leads us to know God, in whom is all wisdom.

This is not a vertical line which takes us out of our relationship to nature and culture into a higher realm of 'spirituality'. Nor is it knowledge first leading to wisdom and understanding, which tends towards the Greek deification of knowledge.

The knowledge of God implies far more than theoretical observation and factual knowledge, available to only a few. It involves the following:

1. Knowing God personally and having a personal, meaningful relationship with him.
2. Knowing God's laws and principles for life and being obedient to them. This includes the areas of personal relationships in the family and the school etc, as well as issues of broader significance such as public justice and a responsible stewardship of the world.
3. Knowing the created world – understanding science and maths.
4. Knowing God as the Creator – imaging him by being creative in all aspects of life.
5. Knowing God's plan for his creation – the story of Man, creation, the fall and redemption.
6. Knowing God's calling – each person's sense of identity and purpose in life.

Thus, apart from the basic skills of numeracy and literacy, all teaching material is approached in an integrated manner, with the focal point being the knowledge of God. The following diagram is a working curriculum model which puts this in pictorial form (figure 4).

Over a number of years we have been greatly influenced by a variety of people in our discussions on curriculum development. In particular we have found the work of Margaret MacIntyre and also Paul Hawkins from YWAM extremely helpful.[1] We have also benefited from books such as *Shaping School Curriculum: A Biblical View* and *No Icing on the Cake*.[2]

As a starting point we take an aspect of the character of God through which he has revealed himself to man, progressing through history. The following example takes the quality of sanctifier, through which he introduced himself to mankind in a covenant manner by calling himself JEHOVAH M'KADDESH – 'The Lord who makes you holy'.

The teachers go through the following process:
1. Meditation and prayer on this aspect of God and all that it means in all of creation.

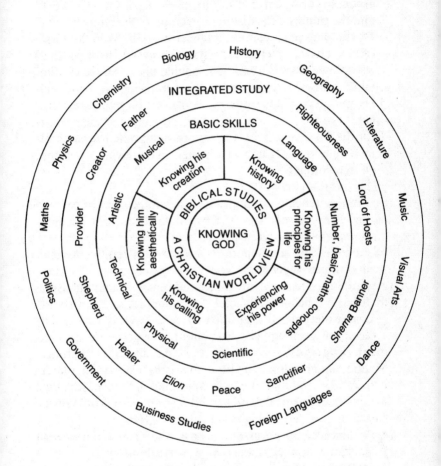

Oak Hill School – Curriculum Model (April 1987)
Figure 4

2. Choosing Scripture passages which demonstrate this aspect of God's nature. This forms the basis for topic work and the material for the memorisation of Scripture.

3. Developing practical teaching matter, initially in the form of flow charts which cover different ways of knowing God as outlined above. These will include historical, scientific, mathematical or aesthetic ways of knowing God and will be material which reflects, contrasts or expresses this aspect of God's nature. This forms the basis of topic work for the following term. Copies are sent home for parental involvement and often the theme can be developed in the church context.

This has the effect of:

(a) Forcing teachers to approach the subject matter from a different perspective. Their analytical faculties become servants to their spirits.

(b) Encouraging teachers to develop a Christian worldview and thus to teach it.

(c) Helping us to dismantle the sacred versus secular dualism.

(d) Learning becomes 'whole'. For example, to learn about water merely in a scientific way, ie as H_2O, is a 'reduced' form of learning. Water should never be reduced to its physical and chemical aspects. It has an economic function, a recreational function, an aesthetic function, etc. It can be a symbol of the Holy Spirit and the seal of forgiveness in baptism. By understanding water in this full sense, we can see something of the heart of God.

(e) Religious Education, as a separate subject, is not necessary. It is implicit in the whole curriculum.

The following passages and flow charts show how this theme was put into practice in the infant department and the junior/middle school department.

Infants' department

In the autumn term of 1987 the core curriculum topic for the school was *Jehovah m'Kaddesh* – 'The Lord who makes you holy'. The teachers in the primary department met together to meditate on Scripture and to pray together. We decided to look at fire as a purifying force and began by considering it as an agent of change. Together we drew up the following flow chart, integrating language, writing, geography, history, science and maths work (figure 5).

In the infants' department the topic started with a large bonfire in the playground, with the children experiencing the sight, smell, sound and feel of fire. With the top infant group we then examined the effect of fire on metal, wax, water and other substances, seeing how it brought about change. As an example of the power and grandeur of fire in nature, we also looked at volcanoes. We discussed the way fire was first used in history among cavemen; we went to visit a fire station and the Industrial Museum. The children recorded what they had found out in paintings, models and creative writing.

As we focused on fire as a purifying force, we found that it affected children personally. In worship times the children experienced God's touch as they responded to verses in Psalm 24:

> Who may ascend the hill of the Lord?
> Who may stand in his holy place?
> He who has clean hands and a pure heart.

As a result of this work children were able to understand the character of God as sanctifier, reflected in all areas of their lives, and begin to experience and know him in this way.

Junior department

In Exodus chapter 31 verse 13 God reveals himself to the Israelites as 'I am the Lord who makes you holy' – *Jehovah m'Kaddesh*. Having thought and prayed independently, we met together as junior teachers to discuss what theme and topic work would bring out this exciting facet of God's character. The work chosen would also have to fulfil the criterion of enthusing the children about God's world and give them some understanding of where and why things have gone wrong.

We felt that sanctification implies change and that although God is the same yesterday, today and tomorrow, he has the power to change situations, institutions, societies and individual people. After prayerful consideration we decided to look at different aspects of city life and consider how things could be changed if we were to put biblical principles into practice. Having decided on the main theme we then considered how other areas of the curriculum could be integrated with this. We believe that integration is a very important aspect of any curriculum, be it primary or secondary, because God created the universe in all its diversity, with laws running through everything and every aspect being dependent on and integrated with the other aspects. The flow chart on page 238 illustrates in some measure the work we covered and how we integrated the different areas of study (figure 6).

Notes

1. Youth With A Mission, 13 Highfield Oval, Ambrose Lane, Harpenden, Herts AL5 4BX.
2. *Shaping School Curriculum: A Biblical View* eds. Geraldine Steensma and Harro Van Brummelen. Grand Rapids: Signal Publishing Corporation, 1984. A series of booklets covering areas such as mathematics, history, language, social studies, integral learning, physical sciences and others. £1.00 each.
   No Icing on the Cake ed. Jack Mechielson. Melbourne: Brookes-Hall Publishing Foundation, 1980. £4.95.
   Both these books are available from the Christian Studies Unit at Widcombe Vicarage, 65 Prior Park Road, Bath BA2 4NL.

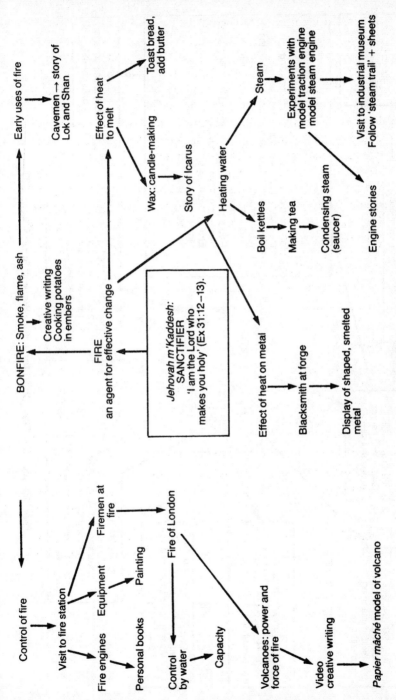

Figure 5

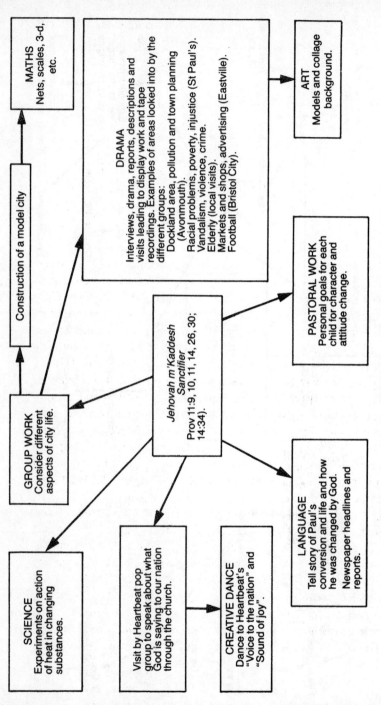

MATHS
Nets, scales, 3-d, etc.

Construction of a model city

DRAMA
Interviews, drama, reports, descriptions and visits leading to display work and tape recordings. Examples of areas looked into by the different groups:
Dockland area, pollution and town planning (Avonmouth).
Racial problems, poverty, injustice (St Paul's).
Vandalism, violence, crime.
Elderly (local visits).
Markets and shops, advertising (Eastville).
Football (Bristol City).

ART
Models and collage background.

GROUP WORK
Consider different aspects of city life.

Jehovah m'Kaddesh
Sanctifier
Prov 11:9, 10, 11, 14, 26, 30;
14:34.

PASTORAL WORK
Personal goals for each child for character and attitude change.

SCIENCE
Experiments on action of heat in changing substances.

Visit by Heartbeat pop group to speak about what God is saying to our nation through the church.

CREATIVE DANCE
Dance to Heartbeat's "Voice to the nation" and "Sound of joy".

LANGUAGE
Tell story of Paul's conversion and life and how he was changed by God. Newspaper headlines and reports.

Oak Hill School – Flow Chart for Junior Work in Spring Term 1987
Figure 6

CONCLUSION

This book opened with my experiences as a supply teacher, conveying the 'spirit' or the atmosphere of a number of (mainly secondary) schools up and down the country. Children and young people often complain of boredom and dissatisfaction. In order to probe this issue we considered the biblical worldview and briefly contrasted this with competing perspectives. In Part 1 we explored the important biblical theme of idolatry and saw that the humanistic worldview of the Enlightenment was idolatrous in the sense that human beings focus upon the created (the worship of science, technology and economic growth) and so forget the Lord and his claims upon our lives. This idolatry refuses to develop culture and civilisation to the glory of God (cultural mandate) but instead encourages man to rule and master 'nature' to the glory of himself.

At this juncture we examined the spirit of the 1980s and saw that the optimistic humanism of the eighteenth-century Enlightenment is being replaced by a pessimistic humanism which tends to stress coping and survival. It seems that the problems of discipline and the crisis in confidence that we are presently witnessing in our educational system are intimately connected to the spirit of our age.

In Part 2 we examined typical textbooks that children read. These textbooks are not unprejudiced or 'value-free' as is often assumed; implicitly and explicitly they transmit a humanistic worldview, be it optimistic or pessimistic. Constant exposure to such material deadens children to such biblical themes as creation, fall, salvation, atonement, justice, miracles, stewardship, wisdom, faith and wholeness. This means that the modern secular curriculum tends to initiate children into an understanding of life that is hostile to the biblical worldview.

Finally in Part 3 we looked at the contribution of Christians who are seeking to rethink and redirect education in the light of a Christian vision of life.

Before we bring this book to a close we need to touch briefly upon the National Curriculum and consider possible courses of action.

The National Curriculum

The National Curriculum, introduced in the 1988 Education Reform Act, lays down three core subjects – English, science and mathematics – and seven foundation subjects – technology, history, geography, music, art, physical education and, at the secondary stage, a modern language. The school's basic curriculum must also include religious education for all pupils.

This new legislation also proposes to test and assess the 'knowledge, skills and understanding' which all pupils of different abilities and maturities are expected to have achieved by the end of each 'key stage'; that is by about the ages of seven, eleven, fourteen and sixteen.

I wish to make three points that I believe are neglected in much current analysis of the National Curriculum.

First, the National Curriculum understands knowledge and understanding as neutral, just like the 1944 Butler Act. The implication is that Christianity (or any other non-Enlightenment religion) has very little to say about the complete curriculum. In short, both Acts presuppose that 'reason' or 'science' can reveal almost the entire curriculum. Religious education is only an extra; it can make no claim to 'truth'. The dominant worldview of the curriculum (humanism) marginalises and trivialises alternative worldviews.

Secondly we would do well to notice that the dominant thrust to the National Curriculum is a pragmatic and utilitarian humanism in contrast to the Act of 1944. Look at this extract from a curriculum working group:

> The use of computer and information technology and other advance technologies in control, simulation and data storage and retrieval is becoming increasingly important in our society. This fact should be reflected in the use of computer and information technology across the school curriculum. Each subject group as it is set up is being asked to consider the scope for using computer and information technology in its subject and to frame appropriate attainment targets.
>
> Pupils should prepare for the world of work by learning how to work in teams as well as by themselves; by understanding the importance of functional efficiency, quality, appearance and marketability; and about the importance of working within financial and technical constraints.
>
> Design and technology are vital areas of the curriculum. They are of great significance for the economic well-being of this country. I believe it is essential that we press ahead quickly in establishing them within the national curriculum.[1]

Terms such as 'control', 'efficiency', 'marketability', 'world of work' and 'economic well-being' reveal a reductionistic and pragmatic humanism. This perspective has been effectively summarised by Brenda Watson:

> that economics is the key to life;
> that technology can control the future;
> that people matter chiefly in so far as they work;
> that the arts, humanities and religion are to be seen largely as pleasant extras, to be accommodated if there is time;
> that there is either no spiritual side to life or if there is it is

unimportant and secondary;
that in the end there is only matter, money and the industrial machine.[2]

It is telling that a National Curriculum consultation document implies that almost half the 'curriculum time' will be devoted to science, maths, technology and English, whereas art, music, drama and design will be relegated to one tenth of the time available![3] This commitment to science, technology and 'the world of work' betrays a pragmatic and utilitarian worldview.

We could say that these emphases in the National Curriculum reflect our modern world's idolatrous allegiance to the gods of science, technology and economic growth. Prevalent in our secular culture is a deep scepticism about meaning, purpose and integration. If the God of revelation is not allowed to reveal himself and his purposes for the human race and his creation, then a religion of coping and industrial adaptation will soon become the only religion on offer. I go so far as to call this utilitarian humanism a religion because as a vision of life it provides its adherents with faith, hope and orientation; man forgets God and places his faith and hope in his rational and technical powers to save him. This religion deadens men, women and children to their true callings; the voice of God, his power, splendour and beauty, are drowned and overpowered by the clamour of secular gods.

Thirdly we need to notice that the National Curriculum tends to understand education in terms of subjects rather than integration. A recent document states, 'The clear objectives for what pupils should be able to know, do and understand will be framed in subject terms.'[4] If testing and assessment is undertaken at the ages of seven eleven, fourteen and sixteen, and if such testing is subject-centred, then there will be considerable pressure for learning to be subject-centred. If teachers are teaching to a 'test', the knowledge and information required will be fragmented, giving a reductionistic and impoverished understanding of the subject as a whole and the interrelationships between different areas of the curriculum.

How can we respond to these many challenges?

I stressed in my opening chapter that the biblical perspective repeatedly emphasises the theme of wisdom. Wisdom brings life and it concerns the obedient response to God's ways. These ways can be summarised in terms of justice, righteousness, compassion, faithfulness, stewardship and wholeness. God's laws are not narrow, lifeless rules that cramp our style! To walk in God's ways brings 'shalom' to men, women, animals, plants, soil, water and air. The kingdom of God is good news for the entire creation. In Luke chapter 4 Jesus preached one of his first sermons. He said:

> The Spirit of the Lord is on me,
> because he has anointed me
> to preach good news to the poor.
> He has sent me to proclaim freedom for the prisoners
> and recovery of sight for the blind,
> to release the oppressed,
> to proclaim the year of the Lord's favour.
>
> Luke 4:18–19

Jesus has come into this world to save people and to restore them. In doing this he proclaims the year of the Lord's favour, a reference to the year of jubilee when destitute and landless people were restored to their land. We could say that Jesus comes, as the King, to renew and save all people and all their many activities and institutions.

These biblical themes of wisdom, salvation and the kingdom of God speak prophetically to education. As Christians we must seek wisdom about education; we must struggle, as a people, to bring the kingdom of God into education.

What might this mean for us? First, we need as parents and teachers to understand the Christian worldview in a much wider and grander sense than we have been accustomed to think. Often we have understood the gospel as private and personal, having little to say about this intricate and complicated world.

But the gospel of Jesus Christ is not small and humdrum; it is not marginal and oblique. It is the power of God to transform. The transformation of people, cities, institutions, theories and shops. The inner renewal of science and technology. Wherever there is distortion, idolatry and misery, the Spirit of Christ longs to proclaim the good news to all creation (Mark 16:15). All of life, in its absurdity, comedy and obscurity can be changed and redirected – to the glory of God.

Parents need to understand the secular worldviews. Then we can help our children to be critical and discerning. This will call for a renewed interest in our children's homework, as well as school work, and a patience to impart wisdom. We can talk with our children and show them that Jesus Christ is Lord of everything; we can open their eyes to the simple biblical truth that Jesus Christ owns this world and that everything in it (including homework) can be transformed through his death and resurrection.

It will also call for parents to take up the growing opportunities to be involved in their children's schools in order to bring wisdom and insight into those situations where they are active. Since the 1986 Education Act there is now an increased number of parent governors who share responsibilities towards the school's provision of the National Curriculum as well as religious education and sex education. With their responsibilities for the management of finance for resources, governors will participate in many decisions that reflect curriculum priorities. Christians in Education has an extensive range of resources and professional consultants to help Christians who are involved in education in a variety of ways.

Christian teachers can read books on worldview and so gain confidence to challenge the idea of neutrality.[5] The Education

Reform Act 1988 requires that the curriculum for maintained schools should promote the spiritual and moral development of pupils as well as other aspects of development. In the light of the fact that the National Curriculum will most likely promote a pragmatic and utilitarian worldview, it is vital that Christian teachers develop a Christian perspective in their teaching; this will indeed promote the 'spiritual and moral development'[6] of their pupils.

We live in a pluralist society and Christians have every right to develop education in the light of their basic beliefs. Boldness to be prophetic will grow and flourish as we experience confidence that we have something coherent and vibrant to say. For too long Christians have felt embarrassed about their views. Why? Because we have understood the gospel in a restricted way. To rediscover the distinctiveness and scope of the gospel is to rediscover boldness and prophetic power. We need to rediscover the radical and comprehensive claims that Christ makes upon our lives. Teachers may find useful the courses provided by the Association of Christian Teachers' Centre.[7] These courses try to help teachers to understand their professional responsibilities in a Christian way.

Secondly, we need to make the most of our present system. We have a semi-pluralist (dual) educational system. This means that our system, unlike the American one, includes over 7,000 church schools, approaching a third of the total school provision. There are voluntary controlled and voluntary aided church schools that are funded by the government.

Sadly, with notable exceptions, such schools often promote a similar understanding of life to the county schools. The assumption tends to be that the curriculum delivers a neutral body of knowledge and RE and assemblies add on the spiritual dimension (although there has always been some awareness of the Christian ethos within a church school). As we challenge neutrality, we can also challenge such schools to be more faithful to a vision of Christian education. Biblical themes of stewardship, coherence, responsible knowing, justice and servanthood could be integrated into the curricula of our Church of England and Roman Catholic schools if sufficient numbers of parents and teachers were prepared to struggle together. This task would require prayer, study, meditation, perseverance, vision and a sense of 'working together'.

Thirdly there are new moves in education which might allow greater plurality of educational options. Within the independent sector of education there have always been schools that provide an alternative education to 'maintained' schools, and many have Christian foundations. New independent Christian schools, set up in the last ten years, are trying to develop Christian curricula. These could develop Christian education in exciting ways but presently these schools are struggling without financial assistance from the government. These schools are also few in number (about sixty) and small in size (most have less than one hundred pupils).[8]

Another new development is the new government policy of allowing schools to opt out of local authority control and become grant maintained. We have yet to see whether this becomes a means by which schools are given the freedom to provide a more apparently Christian education than the county schools. Grant-maintained schools will still be required to conform to the National Curriculum. We need to explore to what extent this commitment to the National Curriculum compels schools to devise curricula that are pragmatic and utilitarian.

Fourthly it may be the case that we should begin to work together towards a different educational system which will allow a genuinely Christian perspective to be provided in schools for those who want it. The Dutch educational system is a good example. In Holland any group of parents may form a school association providing they have at least 50 students for a city whose population is up to 50,000, or 100 students for a city whose population is between 50,000 and 125,000 or more. Parents may send their children to a school in a nearby town if there are not enough children in a given city. The government will pay for any transportation costs. The government also pays for the entire cost of the building and appropriate equipment, lighting, heating, cleaning, textbooks and maintenance.

This means that the national and local governments pay equally for all schools, whether they are state or non-state. Schools are permitted to convey a different worldview from the dominant secularism if that is their wish. Of course, recipient schools must meet certain conditions. They must respect laws regarding teacher-pupil ratios, and teachers must have approved certification. They must also respect a basic curriculum design and make sure that their buildings are safe.

Within these basic frameworks a given school is free to unfold education in the light of its fundamental beliefs, be they utilitarian, traditional or Christian. The Dutch people are very proud of this innovative educational system. A 1971 government publication states:

> The Dutch public regards it as a prized possession because it enables every section of the population to give expression in its own way to the spiritual values that it considers of fundamental importance and to make its own contribution to the development of the community.[9]

This educational system recognises the reality of worldviews and strives to do justice to different groups of people who look at the world in different ways. Such a system certainly does not bring the perfect society, but this educational system does strive to do justice to different faith communities. It does not assume that the light of reason can be preached in every school. Why should the worship of science, technology and economic growth, and the promulgation of human autonomy, be tolerated in every school in the land? Is this just?

As Christians in education may each one of us seek God's kingdom in education. Let us pray that the light and healing power of the gospel will transform education. May the power of God raise up many bold and prophetic people who will seek wisdom and understanding from the Lord. May the words of the prophet Malachi inspire us:

> Then those who feared the Lord talked with each other, and the Lord listened and heard. A scroll of remembrance was written in his presence concerning those who feared the Lord and honoured his name.

Malachi 3:16

Notes

1. *Kenneth Baker announces Curriculum Working Group for Design and Technology* (Department of Education and Science: London, 1987).
2. Brenda Watson, *Education and Belief* (Oxford: Basil Blackwell, 1987), p 11.
3. *The National Curriculum 5–16: A Consultation Document* (Department of Education and Science Welsh Office: London, 1987), p 7.
4. *Ibid*, p 9.
5. See bibliography and in particular *The Transforming Vision* and *Creation Regained*. The Open Christian College provides a worldview course that is an excellent resource for teachers and parents who really want to get to grips with our modern world. For more information write to Carol Holliday (Administrator), 83 Brampton Road, Cambridge CB1 3HJ.
6. See Section One of the Education Reform Act, 1988.
7. Stapleford House Education Centre, Wesley Place, Stapleford, Nottingham NG9 8PD.
8. The Christian schools have recently appointed a National Team. For further information contact David Freeman, The Christian School's Trust, The King's School, New Yatt Road, Witney, Oxon OX8 6TA.

9. R McCarthy, ed, *Society State & Schools: A Case for Structural and Confessional Pluralism* (Grand Rapids: Eerdmans, 1981), p 143.

FURTHER READING

Chalmers, A.F. *What is This Thing Called Science?* Milton Keynes: Open University, 1986.

De Graaff, A.H., & Olthius, J., eds. *Joy in Learning: An Integrated Curriculum for the Elementary School.* Toronto: Curriculum Development Centre, 1973. (An entire curriculum for the primary school.)

Dooyeweerd, Herman. *Roots of Western Culture: Pagan, Secular, and Christian Options.* Translated by J. Kraay. Toronto: Wedge, 1979.

Goudzwaard, Bob. *Idols of our Time.* Translated by Mark Vander-Vennen. Leicester: Inter-Varsity Press, 1984.

—. *Capitalism and Progress: A Diagnosis of Western Society.* Grand Rapids: Eerdmans, 1979.

Granberg-Michaelson, Wesley, ed. *Tending the Garden: Essays on the Gospel and the Earth.* Grand Rapids: Eerdmans, 1987.

Hart, Hendrik. *Understanding our World.* Washington, D.C.: University Press of America, 1984.

Hill, Brian. *Faith at the Blackboard.* Exeter: Paternoster Press, 1982.

—. *The Greening of Christian Education.* Homebushwest, New South Wales: Lancer Books, 1985.

Hobbs, Maurice. *Teaching In A Multi-racial Society.* Exeter: Paternoster Press, 1987.

Illich, I. *Deschooling Society.* Harmondsworth: Penguin, 1973.

Jongsma, Calvin. 'Christianity & Mathematics: Where and How do they meet?' Unpublished paper.

—. *The Shape and Number of Things*. Toronto: Curriculum Development Centre, 1981. An entire mathematics curriculum for the Christian primary school. (CDC 229, College Street, Toronto, Ontario, Canada.)

Kalsbeek, L. *Contours of a Christian Philosophy*. Toronto: Wedge Publishing Foundation, 1975.

Kuhn, Thomas S. *The Structure of Scientific Revolutions*. 2nd ed. Chicago: University of Chicago Press, 1970.

Martin, Charles, ed. *Christian Aims in Education*. Leicester: IVP, 1985.

—. *Schools Now*. Tring: Lion, 1988.

—. *You've Got to Start Somewhere When You Think About Education*. Leicester: Inter-Varsity Press, 1979.

McCarthy, Rockne, ed. *Society, State and Schools: A Case for Structural and Confessional Pluralism*. Grand Rapids: Eerdmans, 1981.

Mechielson, Jack, ed. *No Icing on the Cake*. Melbourne: Brookes-Hall Publishing Foundation, 1980.

Monsma, Stephen, ed. *Responsible Technology*. Grand Rapids: Eerdmans, 1986.

Neuhaus, Richard, ed. *Democracy and the Renewal of Public Education*. Grand Rapids: Eerdmans, 1987.

Newbiggin, L. *Foolishness To The Greeks*. London: SPCK, 1986.

—. *The Other Side of 1984*. Geneva: World Council of Churches, 1984.

Olthius, James. *I Pledge You My Troth: A Christian View of Marriage, Family, Friendship*. New York: Harper & Row, 1975.

Olthius, Jean. *Teaching with 'Joy': Implementing Integrated Education in the Classroom*. Toronto: Curriculum Development Centre, 1979.

Peterson, Michael. *Philosophy of Education*. Downers Grove, Ill: Inter-Varsity Press, 1986.

Palmer, PJ. *To Know as We are Known: A Spirituality of Education*. San Francisco: Harper & Row, 1983.

Polanyi, M. *Personal Knowledge: Towards a Post-critical Philosophy*. London: Routledge & Kegan Paul, 1958.

Poole, Michael. *Science and Religion in the Classroom*. Watford: Association of Christian Teachers, 1984.

Ridderbos, Herman. *The Coming of the Kingdom*. Philadelphia: The Presbyterian and Reformed Publishing Company, 1962.

Russell, Richard. 'Science, Philosophy of Science and Science Education.' Unpublished paper.

Seerveld, Calvin. *Rainbows for the Fallen World*. Toronto: Toronto Tuppence Press, 1980.

Steensma, Geraldine, and Van Brummelen, Harro, eds. *Shaping School Curriculum: A Biblical View*. Grand Rapids: Signal Publishing Corporation, 1984. A series of booklets that seeks to redirect curriculum from a Christian perspective.

Storkey, Alan. *Transforming Economics*. London: SPCK, 1986.

Storkey, Elaine. *What's Right with Feminism*. London: SPCK, 1985.

Wakeman, Brian. *Personal, Social and Moral Education*. Tring: Lion, 1984.

Walsh, Brian & Middleton, Richard. *The Transforming Vision: Shaping a Christian World View*. Downers Grove, Illinois: Inter-Varsity Press, 1984.

Walter, JA. *A Long Way From Home: A Sociological Exploration of Contemporary Idolatry*. Exeter: The Paternoster Press, 1979.

Watson, Brenda. *Education & Belief*. Oxford: Basil Blackwell, 1987.

Wilkinson, Loren, ed. *Earthkeeping: Christian Stewardship of Natural Resources*. Grand Rapids: Eerdmans, 1980.

Wolters, Albert. *Creation Regained: Biblical Basics for a Reformational Worldview*. Leicester: Inter-Varsity Press, 1985.

Wolterstorff, Nicholas. *Educating for Responsible Action*. Grand Rapids: Eerdmans, 1982.

—. *Until Justice and Peace Embrace*. Grand Rapids: Eerdmans, 1983.

Christians in Education

Christians in Education is a registered charity established in 1986 to strengthen the position of Christianity in schools, encourage a biblical perspective on education and serve parents, teachers, governors, schools workers, church leaders and other members of the Christian community who are involved in education.

Education is an area of our national life which is undergoing radical changes and reassessment. While there are growing concerns among many Christians about various educational issues within an increasingly secular system, there are also unprecedented opportunities for a Christian presence in schools. Christians in Education provides the information, training and encouragement that will enable Christians to engage in the spiritual battle that affects the minds and lives of the children of our nation.

CiE's team of professional personnel are available to respond to requests for personal advice and speakers for meetings. Training is provided for school governors and those involved in going into schools to take acts of worship.

To assist schools to build up their resources CiE provides a Video Subsidy Scheme offering a 50% subsidy on over 100 Christian videos for use in schools. A Book Discount Scheme is also available on nearly 200 recommended children's Bible books and general story books.

CiE has a wide range of practical guidelines and information papers on areas such as RE, Multi-cultural Education, Sex Education, the Education Reform Act, Hallowe'en and Being a School Governor. Single copies of these are offered free to CiE Associates. Associates receive a bi-monthly Newsletter about key issues in education as well as information about the publications, courses and services provided by CiE and other organisations.

CiE works closely with other Christian organisations in the field of education. As an active member of the Evangelical Coalition on Educational Issues, CiE participates in corporate initiatives in education and contributes to national government consultations.

For further information about Christians in Education and how to become an Associate, contact:

Christians in Education
16 Maid's Causeway
Cambridge, CB5 8DN